The Powers Manual: A Guide to Benzodiazepine Recovery

By David Powers

The Powers Manual:
A Guide to Benzodiazepine Recovery
Written by David Powers
Edited by Davina Rush

Copyright ©October 2018
Held by David Powers

ISBN-13: 978-1727740523
ISBN-10: 1727740521

Dedicated to Gambit.

*"Anxiety does not empty tomorrow of its
sorrows, but only empties today of its strength."
–Charles Spurgeon*

Medical Disclaimer

The information shared within this book is not intended to replace professional medical advice. Always consult with your physician before making any changes in your treatment or prescription doses. The information within this book is intended to serve as a self-help guide and support for those going through benzo withdrawal. The author takes no responsibility for misuse of information in this book, directly or indirectly, that may result in liability.

Repetition Disclaimer

There are several major themes that are emphasized repeatedly within the chapters of this book. This is because we are working together to create a philosophy for healing within these pages. It is important that at least a few of the most crucial messages within this book really drive home for you, the reader, and resonate with your own vision of healing.

Vocabulary Disclaimer

The goal of this book is to be concise and effective. In order to do this, I took great consideration of my audience and their varying degrees of psychological understanding. While I am certainly adept at writing rigid scientific research, such as this book contains, I do not intend for this publication to be read as a scientific research manual.

Instead, my goal was to sit down with my audience and talk to them from the position of an empathetic human being. Perhaps even as a friend, one that has shared their struggle, but that was able to use his advance knowledge in psychology to create an effective healing strategy from which he achieved profound results for himself.

CONTENTS

Contents continued

Introduction

Yes, you will get better. Yes, there is life after benzodiazepine.

Let's get that out of the way. I know that's the first question on your mind, because it was the first question on my mind when I discovered that I had become dependent to my prescribed benzodiazepine.

In fact, when I began to experience the withdrawal symptoms, I practically ran to my computer, desperate for answers, embarking on a long and exhausting Google expedition. You know the one, it usually begins with WebMD's "you must be dying" and ends up with you watching testimonial videos of people going through benzo withdrawal hell.

Of course, I was quickly overcome by dread once I began hearing the testimonials from people being weaned off of the medication *and* going through absolute torment.

Their symptoms were unreal.
Their stories were unreal.

What makes this even scarier is that many psychiatrists and medical doctors are not familiar with prolapsed withdrawal syndrome. With this condition a person can experience pronounced benzo withdrawal symptoms months or even years after they take their last dose. In many cases, physicians are simply unaware of how debilitating benzo withdrawal can be. They may even confuse your withdrawal symptoms with those of your pre-existing condition.

Unfortunately, these physicians tell you that it's all in your head, that benzo could not be responsible for the bulk of your symptoms. To call it frustrating is an understatement, because you know there's more going on.

Disclaimer: this is NOT an anti-benzo or anti-psychiatry book. The truth of the matter is that, despite the horrible predicament you may find yourself currently in, the medication does help many people, and does have a valuable place in mental health treatment.

That being said, there is a phenomenon taking place regarding serious benzo dependency, with profound withdrawal complications that can last years after an individual has come off the drug. It is a phenomenon that is largely going unnoticed and unaddressed in the field of psychiatry, as well as psychology.

We know this about the drug, about most drugs; after enough exposure, our brains begin to change and we become dependent, experiencing some interesting symptoms. Whatever reason we originally took that drug for (be it to alleviate/treat, or achieve a high), will still be there after the drug. However, now its symptoms are typically more pronounced and distressing.

For example, one of the most common symptoms of withdrawal from a pain pill, surprisingly, is pain. Similar is true with muscle relaxers, where the withdrawal consists of severe muscle tension, even spasm. Similar is true with alcohol, which makes one very social and frees inhibitions, however, its withdrawal creates intense social anxiety.

Benzodiazepine is no different. You likely began taking the medication for some kind of anxiety management. Therefore, at least during your wean and shortly after, you're going to experience heightened symptoms of anxiety.

Understand that. Be prepared for that, but also know this; our brains are perhaps the most fantastic, complex organs of adaptation. Our brains are designed to adapt and to heal. We only need to guide it in the right direction.

This book is a result of my experiences, and my journey into this relatively unknown area of psychotropic-rendered mental illness (that is benzodiazepine withdrawal), and it's ugly manifestations: prolapsed withdrawal syndrome, and agoraphobia.

We will talk more about those later.

I have begun referring to the information that I have collected and am about to share with you here as *The Powers Manual,* which I hope will serve as a comprehensive foundation and framework for understanding benzo recovery.

Previous literature on benzo recovery has largely focused on two things; the benzo basics, and advice on weaning at home. This book differs from those in that it provides a larger rationale, as well as a guide for recovery, managing symptoms and dealing with pre-existing anxiety. Furthermore, my guide encompasses life *after* benzo and how we can continue to manage our anxiety.

With my personal experience and research, I have conceptualized a simple but effective mode of recovery that I am confident can be of great help for individuals going through the benzo wean hell.

I wanted this manual to be short and concise, packed with critical elements for success. Information that is not only verified through my own experiences, and many others, but through an extensive amount of research. I also wanted the information to be laid out in a simple 'go-to' format, so you can jump right to a specific area of interest without digging through pages trying to find what you're after.

I wrote this book in hopes that it would be valuable to someone at any stage of benzo recovery. Whether you're just considering life without the medication, or your doctor has directed you to wean off your benzo. Whether you're in the midst of withdrawal symptoms, as you've been tapering for some months, or you've already weaned fully off the benzo but are still experiencing withdrawal symptoms and pre-existing anxiety.

This manual will encompass benzo history, dependence, withdrawal and life after medication. Additionally, it shares cognitive-behavioral therapeutic techniques that can help profoundly with symptoms and anxiety management.

In the next chapter, I will share my story and outline how I was able to make a full recovery, significantly decreasing my anxiety. I went from an agoraphobic to giving presentations in front of a full panel of clinical psychologists.

However, I imagine you might have some immediate questions, where reading through an entire book may seem daunting. Therefore, I have decided to include a chapter dedicated to answering the most common questions related to benzo recovery, and life after. You can find this section in chapter 3.

My Story

I've heard so many stories since I began my journey away from benzos back in late 2010, and my story doesn't really stand out in the crowd. In fact, many elements may sound very similar to your own.

For me, it began in 2006, when I was undergoing physical rehab for a neck injury that I had sustained in a car accident. As result of this injury, I had severe pain and spasms in the sternocleidomastoid muscle, a large V-shape muscles in the front of your neck that is responsible for rotating your head from side to side.

I tried several modalities, from massage therapy, hot packs, and electrode-stimulation, to muscle relaxers and anti-inflammatory medicines. Nothing really seemed to work, and I was growing very concerned for my health, which created a lot of anxiety.

Finally, someone recommended I try Valium, a member of the benzo family. It had a significant effect. Not only did it do wonders for my muscle spasm, alleviating a great deal of pain and distress, but it also relaxed my mind. My worries and anxieties melted away. I thought I had found a wonder drug.

However, not all that glitters is gold.

After several months of rather low dosages, I decided I didn't need the Valium any longer, so I quit taking it. Cold Turkey.

That was my first huge mistake.

It was day three without any benzo that I had my first panic attack.

I remember it clearly. I was sitting outside on my porch swing, talking with a friend, and laughing at his joke when all of a sudden I felt a strange jolt to my system. As if someone had flicked an anxiety switch on inside my brain, and my skin began burning as if it were on fire.

I jumped to my feet and put my hands up, sort of bracing for anything, yet nothing, as I felt my consciousness shrink back into a tiny cold and dark space, shrouded in the irrational fear of impending doom.

By that time, my friend had noticed and asked if I was okay, but I didn't understand what was happening to me and couldn't answer. I just knew that my heart was racing, pounding intensely as if I had just run a marathon. I was filled with a paralyzing sense of intense, impending doom. It was so overwhelming that I felt as though I might black out at any moment.

It was terrifying, especially because I did not know what was happening to me. Was it my heart? What is a stroke? Was I having some kind of major neurological brain issue?

Within several minutes the symptoms began to fade, and I still had no idea what had come over me. I just knew that it left me feeling shaken.

After speaking with my doctor, I was informed that I had experienced a panic attack, and that I had an undiagnosed anxiety disorder. He explained that up until this point, up until I had quit taking the medicine (cold turkey and without his medical advice), I had been getting anxiety relief from the benzo. Needless to say, I was instructed to continue taking the drug, because I physically and mentally needed it.

This didn't sit well with me because I didn't really have an anxiety issue, that I knew of, prior to taking the medication. Moreover, I did not even begin taking the benzo *for* anxiety in the first place, so how could this be?

Be that as it may, I was indeed receiving physical and emotional relief from the prescription. So, I followed my doctor's orders and kept taking the drug.

A few years went by, and the benzo worked great. However, I began to build tolerance, and the drug simply didn't seem to be working as well as it had in the past. I was instructed by my doctor to raise the dosage. What began as a 2mgs treatment of Valium once a day, had built up tolerance to 10mgs of Valium 1-3x a day.

It was during the very beginning of my bachelor's program in college that I hit what I've come to refer to as, **The Wall**. In short, The Wall was a period where I had upped my dosage over the years to the point that it was no longer safe or wise to increase the dosage any further. At this point, the drug essentially begins to lose its effect, because the brain has now become dependent and is requesting more of the drug to achieve the same effect.

The wall is a period where symptoms of anxiety start emerging again, despite the benzo. At this point the doctors are likely to switch benzos, or now that benzo prescription ethics have change drastically, they may decide to switch you to an antidepressant.

"But I don't have depression," you may be saying?

Antidepressants have been shown in clinical studies to be effective in treatment and management of anxiety symptoms. However, an antidepressant, like a benzo, does nothing to address lifestyle changes, behavioral changes, cognitions and irrational thinking tied to symptoms that are likely to be the culprits of your anxiety. Antidepressants simply and effectively treat symptoms of anxiety.

At this point in my benzo story, I was given Xanax for "breakthrough" anxiety. In other words, I would only use this medication when I felt intense anxiety coming on or needed to thwart off a panic attack. I was also given an antidepressant. I was prescribed this even after I had explained to my doctor how I felt strongly that the benzo was the culprit, creating profound withdrawal symptoms. I was informed that I was mistaking these symptoms of withdrawal with the symptoms of my pre-existing anxiety disorder.

Now, all of this came at a critical point in my life. I had just begun working on my Bachelor program in college, and I had already been working extensively to apply for med school. However, I also had a huge passion for psychology and wanted to provide therapy for others.

This created a crisis of faith for me, the details of which I will not bore you with. However, it is worth noting because the lessons I learned in those biology courses would later assist my recovery.

I did eventually decide to follow my passion and pursue a career in clinical psychology, a decision that also profoundly impacted my recovery from benzos.

In short, I began to realize that the doctors were simply not aware of what was happening to people who were experiencing benzo withdrawal. Particularly individuals that, after years of use, were experiencing rather traumatic and prolonged debilitating withdrawal symptoms. I could see that the only method of treatment for this condition seemed to be either more benzos, or the introduction of other medication, such as antidepressants.

The more I researched and learned about benzo withdrawal, as well as treatment options today, the more I saw the value in weaning off the drug and trying to conquer the anxiety on my own. I was determined to try, and if my plan didn't work, I would surrender to the idea of taking an antidepressant.

I considered it an experiment to attempt tapering off the drug and implementing psychological cognitive-behavioral techniques to manage my symptoms of withdrawal, as well as the symptoms of my supposed pre-existing anxiety condition.

My mind was made up. I was going to wean, but how?

How much? How long would it take? What are the symptoms going to be like and what should I expect? Would I be able to work? Would I be able to finish college? What about my social life, friends, family, and relationship?

My head was spinning, I was anxious, but I felt backed into a corner.

Simply put, my medical method of treatment was no longer working. Not only that, but the literature I was reading about benzo suggested that it was safe and even necessary to wean off the drug after several years of use.

I suppose we can consider it a neurological cleansing, as prolonged use of benzo is associated with some serious health risks, most notably, degradation of memory and cognitive skill.

Of course, some people take benzos for decades and do just fine. That should be noted. Unfortunately, I wasn't one of those people.

After I discovered the *Ashton Manual,* based on the work of Dr. Heather Ashton (a benzo withdrawal specialist), I felt much better about how I was going to handle my wean. Her manual answered a lot of my questions and was packed with a ton of excellent information and resources. I urge anyone reading this to please research Dr. Ashton's work as well, especially her Benzo Withdrawal Manual.

However, as helpful as Ashton's manual was, it still didn't give me all the answers I was after. It did little to help me in terms of understanding and managing my symptoms, nor did it provide me with any kind of direction in the ways I might facilitate my own recovery. Simply put, her manual is a conversion manual on dosages and weaning rates, though it also has a lot of other relevant information on benzo dependence, withdrawal, and recovery.

Although I will be including similar information in this book, that is not my primary focus. While figuring out and achieving a plan for weaning is a must, there are a number of other elements that are critical to our recovery as well.

Getting back to my story, I finished my bachelor's program while weaning, a feat that I almost feel is deserving of an award! To call such an accomplishment "challenging" is a gross understatement.

Paradoxically, it was perhaps the best thing I could have done, to keep myself in the fire of my fears, so to speak.

Every week I had to give a presentation or lecture in front of a group of my peers, and it was always like an out of body experience.

I didn't realize it at the time, but what I was essentially doing was exposure therapy. The environment I was in was a positive one, and it forced me to put myself in uncomfortable spaces, spaces that I otherwise would have avoided like the plague had I been given the choice.

This became a powerful tool for healing, one that we will be dissecting more throughout this book.

Within two years, I had weaned myself down from 30mg of Valium to nothing. It was slow, but it was gradual and steady, which gave me time to adapt. Did it take too long? Perhaps, but had I progressed faster I think the symptoms (and the entire experience) may have been unbearable, and I would have given up on my mission.

After I graduated with my bachelor's degree, I celebrated by weaning completely off benzo, and I enrolled in a Master's program for Clinical Psychology. I was very optimistic at this point, but I was still dealing with prolapsed benzo withdrawal symptoms, even months after my last dose. Additionally, I had become wise to the fact that I did indeed have a pre-existing anxiety condition.

This was around the time when I really began to discover various therapies that would aid in my continuous recovery. Not only from benzo, but from the anxiety disorder that I had been left with.

So, began another experiment.

Could the information and method that I was learning as a future Clinical Psychologist truly be effective for something like anxiety and benzo withdrawal?

I became my own test subject and started implementing techniques from therapies that I had learned, such as exposure therapy, and cognitive reframing. The outcome of this experiment would be monumental to me. Not only did it have an implication on my recovery, but truth be told, I was also nervous about where my opinions would stand afterward. If these therapeutic techniques did not work, would this cause me look down upon psychology in a negative light and lose faith in all I had learned.

How would I go on to work in a field where I treat people using therapeutic techniques that had failed me?

Needless to say, at this point in my training/education, I wasn't completely sure that I trusted the true effectiveness of psychotherapy. And though I had a serious passion for psychology, I was a little skeptical on the treatment outcomes.

During my wean, I used a number things to help aid in my recovery, from physical exercise, and meditation, to direct desensitization through prolonged exposure of various anxiety causing stimulus. We are going to cover all of those things in this book.

My story has two pivotal sections: the wean process and time period, and then life after benzodiazepine.

It was through my training in clinical psychology that I really began to hone in on the techniques that would transform my disposition with benzo, as well as whatever preexisting anxiety and depression I had before taking the medication.

The next two years after I took my last dosage of benzo were critical to my full recover. This was the period of time where I'd really begun harmonizing all of the elements for healing that I needed. It was within those two years that I had recovered so much that the benzo withdrawal feelings became distant memories.

However, I wasn't out of the woods yet.

I still had many issues that I needed to work on in my life. Lucky for me, I had a head start as I'd already begun working on some of those things during my initial wean. In a sense, I was preparing myself for life after benzo. I knew that this challenge would require my faith; I had to believe that I would make a full recovery, but I also didn't want to feel like I had just stepped out of a time chamber and back into my life. Preparing for the transition, during the transition, was key.

The next few years were about conquering my preexisting anxiety and depression, as well as creating and fostering a new healthier lifestyle that promoted positive psychology and mental health in general. There was also a period where I had to conquer the mental fear of life without a prescription, without any safety net.

I had been told by my psychiatrists, that I needed benzos for anxiety management, and that I would always need them. And yet, here I am today, symptom free and without medication; my benzodiazepine withdrawal a distant memory. In truth, the memory almost feels like it happened to someone else. I haven't taken the medication in five years and I deal with less anxiety symptoms now than I have in a long time.

So, I know firsthand that healing is real and that it happens.

I am not here to offer false hope.

I'm not here to tell you that you should wean off your benzo, and I'm certainly not here to tell you to ignore the directions of your physician(s).

This manual is simply a guide and resource to developing and fostering a safe and healthy recovery from benzodiazepine, should you and your doctor decide that coming off the drug is the best course of action. Each case is different.

In short, this manual is a compilation of everything that has helped me to heal during my difficult time, and everything, comprehensively, that I wish I had access to (in one collective resource) when I needed it most.

Quick Checklist of Essential Questions

Q1: What is benzodiazepine?

A1: Benzodiazepine (benzo) is a class of psychoactive drug that is in a family of drugs known as tranquilizers, which act upon the nervous system, producing sedative and anti-anxiety affects. Benzodiazepine is also used as a muscle relaxant and can reduce seizure. Some individuals use the medication to help with sleep disorders, while most people use the drug to treat anxiety.

Benzodiazepines are habit forming and can have adverse effects upon health, such as memory and cognitive decline.

Q2: What is benzodiazepine withdrawal syndrome?

A2: Benzodiazepine withdrawal syndrome (aka benzodiazepine withdrawal) is a myriad of symptoms commonly associated with withdrawal from the benzodiazepine. Typically, the longer the use and the higher the dose, the more pronounced the withdrawal symptoms.

A2: continued...

Benzo withdrawal symptoms include, but are not limited to: akathisia, anxiety, blurred vision, chest pain, depersonalization, depression with possible risk of suicidal ideation, derealization, dizziness, Dysphoria, diarrhea, fatigue, headache, hot and cold spells, hypertension, hypochondriasis, insomnia, night terrors, impaired memory and concentration, mood swings, muscle spasms/cramps, obsessive compulsive disorder, paranoia, perspiration, tachycardia, and panic attack.

Q3: Is benzodiazepine addictive?

A3: Yes, benzodiazepine is habit forming, and one can develop a dependence/addiction. This is a key reason why we have seen a major decline in the number of new benzodiazepine prescriptions. Instead, SSRI's are more commonly used as a first-line treatment for the spectrum anxiety disorders.

Q4: What is benzodiazepine tolerance?

A4: Benzodiazepine tolerance occurs, usually after a prolonged period of exposure to the drug, by which neurological changes begin to take place rending the body more tolerant of the benzo, thereby requiring a stronger dose to achieve the desired effect. Tolerance comes first and can lead to dependence.

Q5: Will I get better?

A5: Yes. You will get better. It will take time and effort on your behalf, but your brain will heal. Prolonged exposure to benzodiazepine biologically alters the brain, but research suggests that these changes do in fact repair themselves after prolonged cessation from the drug.

However, one hugely overlooked aspect of healing from benzodiazepine withdrawal has been and continues to be the role of the pre-existing disorder that came before the individual began taking the medication for treatment of symptoms. The problem is, the benzodiazepine did not cure the preexisting condition, nor did it help you develop coping strategies, nor did it give you techniques you can use to reduce anxiety symptoms.

Therefore, our healing from benzodiazepine dependence is only half the battle.

Q6: How long does this last?

A6: The answer to this question depends on how long you've been taking a benzodiazepine, what doses you have been taking, and how much effort you put into your recovery. If you're going to lay in bed and simply wait for the benzo withdrawal storm to pass, then you're likely to drag out the symptoms, and possibly develop more serious conditions, such as agoraphobia.

That said, if you've only been taking short term (six months or less) then withdrawal is likely to take a few months to achieve, and then we must give ourselves some more time to heal after our last benzo dose.

If you've been taking benzos for one or two years, then withdrawal will be slower, and it will of course take longer, perhaps one year or so of healing.

If you've been taking benzos for more than a few years, and have reached a high daily dose, then withdrawal will be much more difficult, but achievable. For these individuals, withdrawal and healing can take 2-3+ years.

Q7: What if I never get better?

A7: Yeah? And what if a plane crashes into your house while you're sleeping? Or what if a lion escapes from the local zoo and ambushes you while you're walking to your car in the morning for work?! There is no room for "what if's" during the benzo wean and healing process. Erase this notion of possibly not getting better out of your mind, as it will literally harm your recovery.

The bulk of evidence before us on this topic suggests strongly that most people get better, and most people eventually go back to their normal lives. Many people find themselves with a better quality of life than what existed before or during benzo use. It is very achievable, especially with the right work and dedication.

Less than 1% of 1% worst-case benzo withdrawals find themselves still struggling with symptoms 3+ years after their wean. And if they do, it's highly likely that these symptoms are tied more to other factors (such as pre-existing conditions or other conditions that developed during withdrawal) than the benzodiazepine itself.

That said, there are some very rare cases where individuals struggle some years out after their last dose. Could this possibly be tied to neurological damage resulting in long-term benzo use and withdrawal? Scientists are currently researching this exact problem. Hopefully, with more awareness to this rather silent problem we can influence more research and potentially better treatment outcomes.

Q8: But how many people actually get better?

A8: Most people get better, but better is an arbitrary word. What is meant by "better"? Do we mean to imply symptoms improvement tied to withdrawal affect? Then yes, almost ALL people heal from that withdrawal. But if we are asking whether or not we go back to "normal" after getting off a benzo, well that really depends on what normal is and was?

Always keep in mind the reason you first began taking a benzo, as that condition is likely to still be there and will require treatment, be it by other medicines and/or psychotherapy.

Q9: Why can't I sleep?

A9: Because benzodiazepine is essentially a tranquilizer and has a profound affect upon sleep. When you go through withdrawal, symptoms are typically opposite to what the therapeutic effect of the drug was. Where the drug once helped you sleep and it reduced your anxiety, it now interferes with your sleep and creates anxiety.

Q10: How can I sleep?

A10: I do highlight some methods in this book on ways to help promote sleep. These things range from over-the-counter items, such as valerian root, and melatonin, to other ways of achieving relaxation, and conditioning the mind/body to allow for sleep. Unfortunately, sleep disturbances amongst benzo weaning individuals are extremely common, and persistent, even for some time after benzo withdrawal.

Q11: Why doesn't my doctor understand what I'm going through?

A11: This is a huge topic of interest and has been debated for some years amongst mental health professionals of different disciplines, as well as amongst the scientists conducting the research in this area. Depending on whom you ask, you're going to receive some different point of views, but since you asked for mine...

A11 continued... Simply put, your medical doctor may not be convinced that benzo is creating the bulk of your problems. He or she is not evil, they're not out to get you, or harm you. They just may not be convinced that benzo withdrawal is creating all the symptoms.

Additionally, your doctor may worry that too slow of a wean can cause more problems for you than it fixes, and this is a very important point to consider as well. It is also worth considering what your psychiatrist is trained to do.

He or she is not trained (and licensed) in counseling. Nor do most of them today acknowledge or lean toward the holistic psychological model of mental illness. For a psychiatrist, most anyway, anxiety is a chemical problem, and it is solved using chemicals. Just as a psychologist uses talk therapy and is not going to prescribe you meds. Both can be highly effective, and when combined, can be the most effective.

However, attitudes are changing with more and more medical doctors recognizing that benzo dependence can have some long-lasting and seriously negative affects upon the patient. Researchers are exploring drugs that can help reduce withdrawal symptoms, and potentially help speed up the brain's recovery.

We must be careful not to demonize psychiatry, nor psychology, for that matter, simply on the backs of a few misguided or poorly trained physicians.

Q12: What is meant by wean?

A12: A wean is a slow, gradual reduction of a substance until there is no more medicine being taken-- In this case, benzodiazepine. This is important because a slow and steady wean is going to help keep withdrawal symptoms a lot more manageable by reducing drastic spikes in symptom severity.

Q13: How do I wean?

A13: The first step is to consult your doctors and make sure they are on board with your decision and can help you reach your desired outcome. At that point it is wise to speak with your doctor about working out a slow and steady tapering until you are finished taking the drug. The *Ashton Manual* may be of some assistance.

Q14: What is the Ashton Manual?

A14: *The Ashton Manual* is a benzodiazepine withdrawal manual that is intended to help_an individual with their wean, by focusing on a slow, steady and consistent tapering off the medication.

Dr. Heather Ashton, a prominent researcher in benzo withdrawal, wrote *the Ashton Manual* after working with many patients weaning off the medication. Dr. Ashton was one of the first people to recognize the nightmare that many individuals were experiencing as they attempted to free themselves from the unintended addiction. She also observed that the symptoms could be more tolerable if patients would pace themselves by weaning more slowly. However, she also noted that some people still battled withdrawal-like symptoms, even after coming off the drug entirely.

You can find the Ashton Manual online via: https://www.benzo.org.uk/manual/

Q15: Is there something I can take to help with withdrawal symptoms?

A15: Unfortunately, there is no quick fix. This is why I stand firm in my belief that benzo withdrawal is the worst of all drug withdrawals. With most other drugs, there is something you can take to reduce symptoms. You don't get that luxury with benzos. Further, the options that may offer you **some** relief, such as alcohol, will likely only make withdrawal harder.

Q16: What is Titrate?

A16: Titrate is a method of administering a drug in liquid form using a dropper, as with benzodiazepine. This helps to administer a more precise amount of benzo—particularly useful when one gets down to the last couple milligrams.

Q17: Why do many physicians recommend that a patient switch to Valium for the purpose of weaning?

A17: Valium is often preferred due to its long-lasting effects, having a half-life of around 48 hours. This means more of the drug stays in your body longer, requiring fewer dosages throughout the day and creating a more even amount of drug concentration in your body/brain.

Additionally, Valium comes in smaller dosages: 2mgs, 5mgs, and 10mgs, as well as titrate.

Q18: Are there support groups for benzo withdrawal?

A18: Yes. There are some wonderful benzo support forums and websites out there, such as:

www.BenzoBuddies.org
www.Benzosupport.org

Q19: What is it like when a person comes completely off a benzo after a long period of use?

A19: The first things to go are the withdrawal symptoms. Anxiety diminishes, and we begin to feel like our old selves. Sometimes, sleep and anxiety still linger a bit, but eventually they do go away.

The important thing to remember is that for most of us there is some kind of underlying condition that will still need to be addressed (anxiety/depression/stress). We have to be certain to accurately differentiate those symptoms from benzo withdrawal symptoms.

Most people, including myself, have a sense of renewed purpose. We feel physically and emotionally revived. As if we have shed an old heavy coat. Eventually, your time in recovery will seem like someone else's bad memory.

Q20: What can I do about my pre-existing anxiety disorder or depression?

A20: Treatment. Learn as much about whatever your condition is and seek out the best treatments. Outside of that, do your work. Every therapist and psychiatrist is well aware that treatment works best when the patient actively engages in their recovery. For conditions like anxiety, depression, and trauma, I always recommend a good licensed and experienced clinical psychologist, especially one trained in cognitive-behavioral therapy (CBT). CBT is arguably the most effective psychotherapy for anxiety disorders.

Q21: What are the biggest obstacles in the way of my recovery?

A21: Isolation and giving up. We have an instinct to sort of lie down on the bed and just wait out the storm. We'd attempt to sleep it out if we could, just like we do with a cold or the flu. However, this is the worst thing one can do for their benzo recovery.

Anxiety is a quickly consuming fire, as is depression, and both are byproducts of benzo withdrawal. Unfortunately, what typically happens is that a person becomes discouraged by the benzo withdrawal symptoms, and the fatigue knocks them down. They begin laying in bed with the exhaustion and symptoms of anxiety/depression rapidly spiral out of control.

The fatigue increases, and we move less. The anxiety/depression increases, and we move less.

Eventually, we find ourselves developing other conditions, such as severe anxiety (agoraphobia) and depression (with possible suicidal ideation).

Therefore, the best thing that you can do is to stay as active as possible during your wean. Go for walks, get out of the house, interact with others when possible. Try to reconnect with your hobbies and things that you once enjoyed, even when you absolutely do not feel like doing them. Do them for the sake of doing them.

Unfortunately, these things are incredibly difficult to accomplish during our wean, but they are completely necessary and doable.

Q22: What is Protracted Withdrawal Syndrome?

A22: Protracted withdrawal syndrome (PWS) is one of the worst things you want to hear about your benzo recovery. PWS is a rare condition by which benzo withdrawal symptoms can remain for months (even years) after a person's last dose of benzo. Usually, this resolves on its own after a period of time, usually within a couple of years.

Brief History of Benzodiazepines

Benzodiazepines (benzos) have been around for more than 50 years, and have commonly been used to treat anxiety disorders, stress, insomnia, muscle spasms, seizure, and alcohol withdrawal. Developed in the 1950's by Hoffmann-La Roche, the anxiolytic tranquilizer worked miracles on anxiety and sleep, quickly becoming widely prescribed. The Rolling Stones even wrote a song about benzos called *Mothers Little Helper.*

Though extremely effective in treatment of anxiety, benzos have endured a love/hate relationship with mental health professionals across the board. As research has grown over the years since benzos first arrived on the scene, the medical community has become increasingly aware of a huge consequence in its prolonged use; tolerance and eventually dependence.

During the last 20 years, abuse rates have skyrocketed to the point that the medical community was forced to reexamine the drug and make some changes. And while abuse rates did climb, we also couldn't deny the positive health benefits of benzodiazepine.

The same can be said about opiates. There is currently a massive epidemic of opiate abuse and overdose. However, opioids are necessary for severe pain relief, and do help millions and millions of people each year.

The topic was never a question of 'should we get rid of benzos', but rather, 'how do we make them safer?'

The problem with benzos was that they worked a little too well, as they tended to create a euphoric high, especially when taken in higher dosages. This caused more people to abuse their prescriptions, and therefore created a street-demand for illegally obtained benzos.

Additionally, benzos react differently, often adversely, with other chemicals. For example, it is very dangerous to combine benzos with opiates, or alcohol, as both can be fatal. In fact, recent research suggests that 75% of recent (2010) benzodiazepine overdoses involved opiates and alcohol.

With enough evidence to warrant a safer approach to benzos, many changes were made regarding their prescriptive use and rate at which they were prescribed. Today, most psychiatrists turn to an antidepressant, such as an SSRI, as a first-line defense in treatment for anxiety.

However, many people are still being prescribed benzos. It is important to note that most of the people who take this medication do not experience the severe withdrawal syndrome that we are exploring in this book. This has to be said in order to give some perspective on the topic, as the internet paints a very distorted picture of benzo, claiming this medication leads to nothing but dependence and withdrawal.

That being said, benzo dependence and withdrawal syndrome are still much more common than perhaps a number of medical professionals are aware of or would care to address.

Benzo & Brains

I won't bore you with tedious information about benzodiazepines and how they interact with the brain, as that information is quite extensive. There are plenty of resources available, should you desire to explore the intricacies of this topic.

However, what I would like to convey at this point is simply a fundamental interpretation of what a benzo is and what it does to our brains. Keep it simple.

So, here's some of the good, the bad, and the ugly.

As I have already illustrated, benzos have a unique effect on our body. If there's one neurotransmitter to remember here, it's GABA (gamma-aminobutyric acid). Benzos effect GABA, which results in sedative, hypnotic, and anxiolytic effects upon the body. In other words, it helps us sleep, relaxes us, and has an anti-anxiety affect.

This is wonderful as a treatment, but much like other drugs, prolonged use tends to change us, biologically speaking.

Over time, our brain begins to adapt to the

chemicals we have introduced into our nervous system, which can result in organic changes in the brain itself. The same is true for other drugs, both psychotropic and recreational.

If we take a drug long enough, it will impact our actual body chemistry. However, if you take away the drug, typically, with enough time and resources, the brain does repair itself.

The thing I want you to take away here is that our brains are very sensitive to chemical alterations, and prolonged chemical use leaves our brains changed. However, most (if not all) of this change *is* reversible, depending on the severity and length of use/abuse.

When one discontinues a drug, often the withdrawal presents itself with the opposite symptoms for which you were initially treated. In other words, if you abuse opiates for pain, then you are likely to experience an increase in pain during the withdrawal process. If you abuse alcohol because it relaxes you and frees your inhibitions, then guess what happens when we remove alcohol from the equation— Restlessness and social anxiety. The same is true with benzo withdrawal. When you think of it this way, a lot of the withdrawal symptoms make sense. Of course, anxiety, inhibition, and fear are going to arise.

On the topic of brain and benzo, I'll leave you with this reminder. Our brains are amazing, intricate and complex displays of adaptation. Trust in your biology. Within your biology is a biological program that is constantly attempting to stabilize and repair itself. Trust in your biology.

Tolerance vs. Dependence vs. Addiction

Tolerance and addiction; two terms that are commonly mistaken, often interchangeably used where perhaps they shouldn't be. I've heard a lot of stories from people going through benzo withdrawal, and opiate withdrawal. People who were taking their legally, ethically prescribed medications for a prolonged period of use and subsequently developing a dependence.

However, they still refer to themselves as "addicts". You can actually see the shame in their eyes, and sometimes hear it in their voice, read it in the words they use to describe themselves and their situation.

They feel terrible about themselves, depressed even.

This label is inaccurate, for two major reasons.

Firstly, you are not an addict, unless you were abusing the drug to get high. In fact, you might not have even really experienced a high at all. Tolerance can set in regardless of whether or not you had a good time on the drug. It's very simple. You introduce a chemical that stimulates a neurotransmitter long enough in the brain and biological changes will undoubtedly occur.

The chemicals do not reach the brain and then the synapses stop to ask, "hey are you high? Do you feel good? Did you abuse this chemical?" They are completely indifferent. They open up and take in as much as they can.

Secondly, be very aware of the difference between *dependence* and *addiction*. If you're experiencing dependence and yet still labeling yourself as an addict, then you're doing yourself a great disservice. This is a negative and untrue narrative that could hinder your recovery. By contributing to a wall of self-defeating talk—the kind of talk that is absolutely common with benzo withdrawal—you are further crippling yourself with unnecessary shame.

Tolerance is bound to happen regardless if you've abused the drug, or even gotten high on it. Abuse is characterized much more by the behaviors, motives, and thoughts surrounding the medication. If you're stealing money to get high, or taking the drug to forget your problems, then perhaps you *are* abusing the drug. Just remember, the brain doesn't know the difference. It just knows chemicals. The important thing is that you recognize the issue and address it.

The Wall

Oh, the Wall. The tallest of walls, of any wall I've ever had to climb. And we can't move the wall, nor go around it, nor go through it. We have to climb it. At some point we were driving along down the benzo brick road, when we came around a bend. We were busy focusing on the details of our life and all of our plans, when all of a sudden, we ran smack into a massive stone wall.

At some point, we come to realize that the signs had been there for a while.

We had driven past various stones in the road, typically to one side or the other— and to which we likely paid little attention. These stones got larger and larger. I guess it made sense that we would eventually hit the wall.

The wall comes when essentially, you've reached the highest dose of the drug that you can take, as advised by your doctor. You leveled off for a while, but now you're experiencing those old symptoms again, the common symptoms you experience just before your doctor tells you to, "up your dose…"

The problem is, this time you can't go up any further.

What do you do? Every week that goes by, the meds work less and less, however your brain is dependent.

Your brain may now be easily processing enough benzo to tranquilize a small elephant, yet it has little to no noticeable effect upon you.

Now what? You've taken a drug for X amount of time, at X amount of mgs, and you just hit the wall.

The wall is the cold harsh truth that this is no longer working, and something needs to change.

I didn't see the wall before I hit it. I didn't even realize there could be a wall. This is something that bothers me about psychiatry today. So many doctors do not thoroughly inform their patients of the long-term potential affects from the drugs they are prescribed.

First comes the wall, and then comes confusion.

A Few Words on Symptoms

You've seen the list of unbelievable symptoms, and I'd challenge you to find another chemical withdrawal that presents more symptoms, as it is rather unbelievable.

It begins with anxiety, or possibly depression. Anxiety/depression is the base from which all other symptoms emerge and manifest. It is the body of this chemically imbalanced beast.

There are two types of symptom phenomenon that I'd like to highlight.

First are the symptoms that stem directly from the chemical imbalance. Things like anxiety, tinnitus, metallic taste in the mouth, insomnia, nightmares, spasms, rapid heartbeat, and disassociation, to name a few.

The other set of symptoms emerge as a result of the pre-existing anxiety/depression condition (assuming you fall into this category. It's likely you do to some level).

So, essentially, we are fighting two battles, which is a major theme in this book.

We are fighting the symptoms that existed prior to us taking a benzo (and likely the reason we began taking a benzo) and then there's the whacky, horrible, chemical withdrawal itself.

Further, the withdrawal symptoms are so stressful that it typically exacerbates and negatively influences the pre-existing conditions and symptoms, manifesting things to new levels of disorder.

This is when we see a preexisting General Anxiety Disorder become something more serious, such as developing into a panic disorder, and/or agoraphobia. We will talk much more about this in the upcoming pages.

Another piece of information you may find useful, depending on where you currently are in your wean (just starting, half way through, or post-benzo), is that symptoms come and go, often in pairs and even clusters.

For me, it seemed like things changed almost every few months. I basically went through the entire spectrum of symptoms at some point throughout my benzo wean.

You will know that you're really beginning to heal once you feel those stranger symptoms start to disappear, things like: tinnitus (ringing in ear), muscle spasms, nightmare or night terrors, rapid heart-beat or fluttering in the chest and, of course, fatigue. I find that in most people these symptoms are the first to disappear.

The bigger things that you are likely to be left with, even after your last dose of benzo, include general/social anxiety of varying degress, panic disorder, depression, insomnia or other sleep disturbances, and possibly even agoraphobia.

On top of that, we have what I would call disturbances in self-perception that often stick around. This could be a range of things, from poor/negative self-image, poor self-esteem, or a lack of self-belief, to more pronounced things like obsessive-compulsivity.

This makes sense considering all an individual goes through while weaning. It wreaks havoc on our physical, mental and emotional health. The prolonged stress alters our perception of self and the people around us, even the world at large.

We can easily become very negative, very pessimistic and gloomy.

Benzo withdrawal can literally alter our personality.

On the other hand, healing from benzo and triumphing in your fight can strengthen your character and build self-esteem.

We need not succumb to our disposition.

We hit the wall, and that wall is made up of dependence and withdrawal symptoms, as well as symptoms of our preexisting condition. And we *must* climb this wall.

The Thing About Panic Attacks

Here's the thing about panic attacks— though completely frightening, it is usually the first symptom that really triggers us to take a closer look at our situation.

And while it's typically the symptom we first notice, it's not the first symptom we experience after hitting the chemical wall of dependence. Those initial symptoms went unnoticed. They were very subtle, small daily increases of general anxiety, stress, irritability, mental fog, and fatigue.

There were subtle changes in our perception of self, of other people, and the world around us. It was these subtle changes in our thoughts and behavior that came before nature's biological alarm, aka, *panic attack*.

Pay attention to patterns and thoughts, even places that trigger panic attacks. This is important because often it is the case that whatever was associated with the initial attack, be it a symbol or a location or a stimulus, will likely become cemented into the condition, and serve from there forward as a trigger.

This is a two-part phenomenon. It either stems from a cognitive or emotional trigger (such as having a panic attack after someone mentions death), or from an environmental trigger, such as a panic attack in an elevator.

Let's look at the elevator as an example.

One day you're feeling just fine. You get into an elevator and you're minding your own business when suddenly you feel an overwhelming sense of intense fear and impending doom come over you. You then experience a full-blown panic attack in the elevator.

Now, this panic actually stemmed from something much larger in your life. For this example, let's say it was intense anxiety over an impending potential life change. This triggers a panic attack in your subconscious, which you then experience in the elevator, and thus are likely to continue to attribute to elevators.

Another relevant example; you're driving in your car and you experience a panic attack. You then begin to worry about future panic attacks when driving, as you have come to associate driving with the panic attack.

Fear has a way of getting away from us, and of course it loves to dance with other fear; it's drawn to other fear.

However, you must also remember that fear can be a friend. In nature, fear exists to remind us that something is wrong and that we need to make changes. It is a messenger of both good and bad news.

Your panic symptoms should reduce greatly as you heal from benzo dependence and withdrawal. Some of us still experience panic after our last dose of benzo, but that typically is a result of the pre-existing condition.

Whatever the reason, it is treatable.

The Confusion

First the wall, and then comes confusion. What is happening? Why doesn't the benzo seem to work anymore? Why is my anxiety worse than ever? I'm not sleeping. I can't focus. I'm having bizarre dreams. I'm overly emotional. I'm constantly worrying, and I feel like I'm shrinking.

Maybe my doctor knows…

You talk to your doctor and he tells you that it's time to try another drug, maybe an antidepressant. So, you follow his orders while, at the same time, he also instructs you to quickly wean off the benzo (typically within a few weeks), to start the antidepressant.

This is complicated for two reasons. With one drug (benzo), which has caused biological changes in the brain due to chronic use, we are coming down. With the other drug (SSRI), we are going up. Additionally, we are gambling with the symptoms and side effects of two different drugs.

In addition, as if this roller coaster ride isn't frustrating enough, it is very likely that your doctor will dismiss any discomfort that you are going through. I have been overwhelmed by the amount of reports that I've received regarding psychiatrists not acknowledging their patient's benzo withdrawal syndrome. I cannot fully express the amount of frustration that this creates. It is perhaps the most frustrating thing of all, to be told by your doctor that it's all in your head.

That the symptoms you're experiencing are related to your preexisting condition and nothing more.

And to that notion I ask, but what about tinnitus (ringing in the ears) and metallic taste in the mouth? These are two symptoms associated with benzo withdrawal, and *not* anxiety alone. Two symptoms that can emerge years after a patient has completely come off a benzo? Are these symptoms alone not enough to demonstrate that in some rare cases benzo can have a prolonged or prolapsed withdrawal effect? Perhaps it is the term "withdrawal" that stumps medical doctors.

Nonetheless, there is a very real phenomenon-taking place with benzo withdrawal symptoms, and it's hurting many people each year around the world. Denying the problem and   putting the burden on the patient, are not acceptable answers.

So many stories that I've heard over the last several years from individuals recovering from benzo dependence have been quite similar to the example I just shared.

First came the wall, and the symptoms. Then came the confusion, which left us scrambling for answers to our condition. We consulted with our doctors, and then we consulted the internet. It was likely on the Internet that we first got wise to the true nature of our condition.

Each case is different though. Many psychiatrists assist their patients with tapering off the drug. They may prescribe them an antidepressant, or they may recommend therapy.

However, if you're reading this book now then it is highly probable that you are, for whatever reason, going through benzo dependence or withdrawal.

The Decision

After the smoke clears from the confusion stage, and we've begun researching our condition, talking to our doctors and to other people that have gone through similar things, we are faced with difficult decisions.

What to do? Do we switch benzos? Do we add an antidepressant? Should we wean off the benzo? And what the hell do we do about sleep?

Now, at this junction I want to be **VERY** clear about my intentions with the information I am sharing in this book. While I am sharing a benzo withdrawal and recovery guide of sorts, I am in **no way** suggesting that you should wean off your benzodiazepine without consulting you physician first. I do not know your actual situation, and I am not your doctor. I would never play doctor through a book, particularly with something so serious.

IF you're considering coming off of the benzo, please consult your doctor. Get him/her on board first.

I **am** telling you to do your research, consider your options, and to be very careful in whatever direction you choose to go.

The important thing, no matter what your decision, is to realize that treatment and healing are going to be multidimensional and will encompass a number of critical elements in your life. No one pill will cure all anxiety, just as no talk therapy is going to cure all biological dispositions.

Do you need meds? Maybe. Can you wean off, heal, and learn psychological techniques to help you manage symptoms and forge a healthier, less anxious life? In most cases, absolutely!

The decision is yours and it's a tough one. And let's be honest, it's a scary one.

Maybe you trust your doctor, or maybe a bad physician has burned you. Maybe you have a great therapist, or maybe a bad therapist has burned you. There are many factors to consider here. I cannot advise you either way, but I have shared some of my story with you in hopes that it will help.

The Role of Your Psychiatrist

The role of your psychiatrist is to help you feel better. However, they also need to listen to their patient, and not attempt to play God in making crucial decisions for them, especially if the patient isn't on board. I mention this because I've heard many stories where a psychiatrist simply refuses to help their patient wean off the meds. Insisting instead that it's not the meds presenting the symptoms, but rather, the patient's pre-existing condition, or possibly some new manifestation. As we've mentioned before, this is just offensive.

The role of your psychiatrist is to help you achieve your mental health goals, as much as realistically possible. Their medical training should offer you a sense of comfort and safety.

During your wean, the psychiatrist will be able to adjust doses for you so you can achieve a slow and steady taper. We will talk more in later chapters about dosage increments and the possibility of choosing a more ideal benzo (such as Valium) for tapering. This will be important, so that you can continue to break down your meds into smaller consistent milligrams, as this helps tremendously in achieving a smooth detox. If we go too fast, symptoms flare up drastically.

The Role of Your Psychologist

The role of your psychologist is to work with your psychiatrist in helping you to achieve your mental health goals. They are not there to bash psychiatry or insert their opinions on healing. They are there to be effective for you and serve what you need.

The role of your psychologist is to help confirm previous existing diagnosis. Ask yourself, did the psychologist recognize that you had always dealt with anxiety, or did they somehow miss that because they were too focused on symptom management? I've found that this is often the case with lesser-trained therapists, such as those educated at the master's level. I always insist people go with a licensed Clinical Psychologist. One must have a PhD and licensing in order to call him or herself a psychologist.

In my experience, this can make a lot of difference. It is a very serious matter after all. It is very sensitive and if not done properly can result in some terrible outcomes, sometimes fatal outcomes. The golden rule is to always go with the best and most highly trained physician that you can afford.

Additionally, your psychologist will help you learn to identify irrational thinking and self-defeating thought patterns.

You might be thinking, "well gee, I could do that myself and save $$$". Sure, you could, but I'm talking about things that work on a level you simply are unconscious to. That's how they work. The mind is very clever in that way. If our mind made those things conscious we'd no longer be able to use them as a defense mechanism to protect ourselves. There is a cost for that wisdom.

However, the defense mechanism of the unconscious can also hurt us when it becomes excessive and it blinds us from seeing a particular truth. In fact, one might say this is how delusions are born.

Psychologists will help you manage symptoms, identify irrational thoughts, change behaviors and cognitions to promote better health. They can also help with life management tasks, resources,etc.

So please, get all the help you can. You should not do this alone.

Psychology vs. Psychiatry

This is an important area of discussion, and I wanted to hammer on this topic a bit. I do not want to risk presenting this manual in such a way that it seems I had a dog in the fight—as there are plenty of pro-psychology and anti-psychiatry self-help books on the market.

I don't see mental health treatment in those terms; it's not us vs. them, psychology vs. psychiatry. That is a misinformed and outdated perception. Like a team of surgeons, mental health physicians should be able to work in harmony with one another to achieve positive outcomes.

The role of your psychiatrist/psychologist is to help you get better, but also to respect your rights and dignity. Your treatment is ultimately up to *you*.

I've experienced a lot of elitist attitudes in the upper realms of academia, medicine and psychology. I guess it's too easy to go all-in on the stock for which you've invested your life. However, if you are a physician, this should not hinder your ability to effectively treat your patient. This happens to psychologists and psychiatrists alike.

In psychology, we often say, "tailor the treatment to the patient, and not the patient to the treatment."

Reminds me of another saying, "When all you have is a hammer, everything looks like a nail."

So, a word of caution; be skeptical of rigid fundamentalism in any of your doctor's methods. If your psychologist is trying to convince you that psychiatry is bad and that medicines are terrible, then be skeptical of this person. If you're psychiatrist doesn't acknowledge the dynamic role your life, your thoughts and behaviors have on your condition (including your chemistry), then again, be skeptical of that person.

The cardiovascular surgeon works in harmony with the brain surgeon. The psychologist (talk therapist) should work in harmony with the psychiatrist (med prescriber).

It's important to have both of these physicians on the same page and in good communication with each other, aware of the situation at both ends.

I cannot stress how much it bothers me when I hear the countless (majority) of stories involving people weaning off benzo, having a hell of a time, without a psychologist helping them. In my experience, during the wean period, the psychological help was by far the most beneficial, if only because there was nothing the med doctors could do for benzo withdrawal.

If you're coming off of an opiate and having horrible withdrawal, your doctor can give you a pill that will help curb those horrible side effects. However, you currently cannot do that with benzos.

There is no miracle pill that will reduce the symptoms of benzo withdrawal.

While that currently remains an unfortunate fact, there are some promising things, chemically speaking, that scientists are researching. Flumazenil is one such chemical that researchers have been exploring as a treatment for benzodiazepine tolerance and dependence. This particular medication appears to have some real value. In fact, it is considered the gold standard in Italy for the treatment of high-dose benzodiazepine dependency. Hopefully, this will soon become part of standard benzo treatment in the United States as well.

For now, we are kind of on our own in terms of symptom management, but there are things psychotherapists can help with.

For example, there are things that can be done to assist with symptom management, help in identifying irrational thinking, and help changing behaviors that will foster healing.

We will talk more about these things later.

To reiterate, it is not psychology vs. psychiatry.

The ideal picture is to have both of our physicians (psychiatry & psychology) working in harmony. And believe me, we really do need both. A good cognitive-behavioral therapist can do wonders.

The Fear

I remember the fear very well, though at this point my self-attachment to that memory has faded considerably. I remember feeling utterly and totally lost, as if I had been broken neurologically and would never return to normal. I held on in my dark, cold little tower of a bedroom, fatigue stricken, and worry stricken, frazzled to the point of emotional exhaustion.

I remember dissociating one night. I felt as if I had died, that I had left my body, and was hovering in the corner of my room. It was the worst feeling I have ever had. If there were one level above panic attack, this was definitely it.

The myriad of symptoms went on and on and on, day after day, month after month.

Symptoms would often change.

Ringing in the ears one month, then it would stop. Muscle spasms and nightmares the next month, then it would stop, and some other cluster of symptoms would emerge.

The more I endured the more fearful I became that I was never going to be normal again. I would never be able to finish college. I would never be able to work— hell I couldn't even drive my car for a period of time, because I had too much panic and agoraphobia.

It leaves one feeling hopeless and broken, and that's a VERY critical moment for us because it is that attitude that will cause us to lie down and give up.

Segway.

The Worst Thing We Can Do During Our Wean

This leads us to one of the most important topics in this book. In fact, I'm going to repeat it twice.

The worst thing we can do during our benzo wean is to GIVE UP, LIE DOWN, and attempt to SLEEP IT OFF.

I said— the worst thing we can do during our benzo wean is to GIVE UP, LIE DOWN, and attempt to SLEEP IT OFF.

This is an isolating and self-defeating attitude that can only bring us harm, and further from healing.

Firstly, if you're benzo weaning, you're probably not sleeping. Therefore, you are just lying in bed. I've been there. Sometimes it's all we can do, but we still must fight the good fight. The problem with just lying there in bed is that the anxiety symptoms drastically and quickly manifest, getting out of control. You'll go from social anxiety to full agoraphobia (or mild depression to major depression) in a matter of months if you're not careful.

Yes, there is fatigue, and it is horrible, but we MUST fight it.

Yes, our thoughts are negative, and we feel hopeless at times, but we MUST fight it.

This is a temporary war. The more we give, the sooner it ends.

Get out of bed. Get out of your house. The more active you are the less fatigue you will experience. Doing this, you will also be greatly supporting your neurological recovery. Exercise promotes many positive reactions in the human body.

Manifestations of Anxiety: Constant Worry

As we've learned, anxiety and stress can create havoc on our system. We can experience anxiety/stress in our stomach, chest, head, and just about our entire body. It's constantly there and unfortunately it is part of the weaning process. Eventually we become consumed by the worrying: worrying if we're going to get better, worrying about our health and our family, worrying about our careers and future.

Worrying is fear and dread over something that hasn't happened and likely will never happen.

Worrying doesn't remove our suffering tomorrow. It simply robs us of today, which is all we have.

But that's not what our body and our mind convince us of, oh no. There's not much room for rationality through the eyes of anxiety.

There's a reason we can spend hours staring off into space, lost in our head, locked in some mental mathematical equation, that if only we could solve then we could somehow correct our situation.

We think of ourselves as being responsible adults. This is why we are sitting here, stomach in knots, combing over the same handful of variables, over and over and over again. We are being responsible. Right?

Well actually, no we are not. What we *are* doing is getting caught in a mechanism of mind, a hiccup, if you will. It's largely involuntary, a kind of worrying-loop that we get stuck in.

This is necessary for a short period of time, sure. When we have problems, we do need to take time to reflect on those problems, examine them from different perspectives, and explore possible ways that we can correct the problem. However, it's only necessary until we solve the problem. After that, we must confide in our choice and find some peace.

In most things, that is exactly what we do, but not with anxiety, especially irrational anxiety created by withdrawal.

This is why we must be extra careful in paying attention to our thoughts and what we are focused on. When need be, we have to be able to put certain thoughts down and walk away.

Due to the nature of what you are going through, you will have to do this a million times, but please do it a million times if that's the case. You must learn to put down the irrational thoughts. If nothing else, learn to take short breaks, little vacations from the chronic worrying.

Of course, our most constant worry, out of a list of worries, is the worry that we will never get better. You can dwell on this so much that you'll have yourself convinced it's hopeless, you'll have your head spinning and your stomach turning.

We have to be smarter than our brain.

Think of all your constant worrying as chronically biting your nails. You find yourself doing it, and you know you should stop, but struggle. Sometimes you stop immediately, other times you kind of dig a little harder, almost in some last minute extra obsessive attempt to achieve one more anxious gnaw.

Biting our nails is a physical expression of that incessant obsessive loop in the mind.

Worrying is an obsession, and it does more harm than good.

Hypochondriasis

When a person obsessively worries about their health long enough they can begin to internalize their fears. You may develop a sense hyper vigilance, constantly in a state of enhanced sensory awareness. Basically, stimulus tends to be interpreted in exaggerated and threatening ways that are untrue.

For example, you drink a little caffeine and a few minutes later you feel a flutter in your chest. Instantly you think about your heart, and your mind is off and running.

Is it my heart? Has the stress that I've been under with this withdrawal and recovery finally taken its toll on my body!

The anxiety comes rushing in like a tidal wave.

In my own situation coming off benzo, I had already been a bit of a hypochondriac. I was the kid that sometimes came home from school convinced he was dying of some rare disease he'd heard about in class. In conjunction with my imagined illnesses, I also had some very real injuries and health concerns over the years that reinforced the obsessive worry regarding my health.

That's usually how the line gets blurred.

Needless to say, this did not help my taper at all.

Every new symptom that I experienced was quite startling for me. I'd find myself up late at night researching symptoms that came with my withdrawal, though I had somehow convinced myself that they were actually symptoms of something more serious, something unrelated.

I'd think, No. This fluttering in my chest and this insane tension couldn't be from the stress and anxiety of weaning off benzodiazepines, I must have atrial fibrillation!

And this mental fog, no way that's from the depression and anxiety. I must have something wrong with my brain, something more serious!

This all ended for me about midway through my taper, after I remembered **Occam's razor**. Occam's razor was something that I had learned about in one of my philosophy courses, a problem-solving principle. Simply put, the most logical answer is usually the most correct.

For example, you just had some coffee and now you're feeling a fluttering in your chest. Before you give into a panic attack, ask yourself, is it a heart problem or could it be caffeine related?

Which is more plausible?

We talk our self off the ledge with reason and logic.

This may seem overly simple, but it can quickly help us get out of our own way and prevent an avalanche of anxiety.

And remember, the voice of anxiety is never rational or simple. It lies to us. It's like wearing red tinted glasses.

Prolonged Anxiety:
Social Anxiety & Agoraphobia

The most common and debilitating symptom of benzodiazepine withdrawal is anxiety. Social anxiety and agoraphobia are both manifestations of prolonged anxiety. However, anxiety operates on a kind of spectrum, sliding from social anxiety (minor/moderate) to severe panic attack, obsessive-compulsivity and agoraphobia (debilitating anxiety). Agoraphobia may be the worst manifestation of a benzo withdrawal.

In this case, your withdrawal has created such an anxiety and chemical imbalances that you're now in a position where you cannot even leave your own house. You become a prisoner of your own home. Even walking to the mailbox can cause panic attacks and terrible stress responses; pounding heartbeat, blurred vision, dizziness, headaches, and stomach discomfort. The list goes on.

At this point of prolonged stress, many people can no longer work or effectively manage their life. This is a terrifying experience. Most people will never know what it feels like to be disabled on this level, unable to hold a job, drive a vehicle, or even leave their home.

I mention agoraphobia multiple times in this book, and I almost always follow it up by making a point on the importance of confronting our fears, because this is key in defeating anxiety. If you think you're experiencing agoraphobia, then you should act immediately.

You can begin by simply walking to the mailbox daily. Perhaps just once a day for a week, depending on what you can handle. Then, the next week, make it 3 daily trips to the mailbox and back to the house. Do this for a week or two and see how you're feeling.

Then, when you're ready, walk up the street a few houses and back home every day for about a week or two. If you have a pet, take him/her for a walk with you. Eventually, you can walk to the stop sign and back, or around the block and back.

Go further and further, slowly, allowing your brain's flight or fight response to settle and adapt. Little by little, day-by-day, distance-by-distance, the symptoms begin to fade. In fact, all symptoms begin to fade.

The key importance here is in setting goals: hourly, daily, weekly, monthly.

Prolonged Stress:
PTSD & Physical Ailments

Here's the biological rub. The thing we need to do in order to get better (taper off benzo) is also a thing that inevitably creates another similar disorder for us (re-emerging and manifesting mental illness).

The effects of prolonged stress are well researched by this point. We understand how incredibly negative stress is on the body.

We have a term for it, "the silent killer."

Stress typically comes and goes, but when it remains for too long, serious health problems arise.

Weaning off a benzo is nothing short of prolonged stress, and prolonged anxiety.

To put this in perspective for others, I often tell them that benzo withdrawal is the worst chemical withdrawal currently known to man. It's worse than heroin. When a person is detoxing from heroin, or opiates for that matter, they can be immediately taken off the drug and they will not die—though they might feel like they are, and some might even wish they were, but they won't die.

However, people *do* die each year due to benzodiazepine withdrawal.

The brain becomes so dependent on the drug, that after enough time, it can produce fatal seizure activity.

Alcohol is very similar (chemically speaking) and can also produce potentially fatal seizures during severe withdrawal. In fact, alcohol is a very common replacement for benzo, as alcohol and benzodiazepine affect the brain in very similar ways. This is why doctors often prescribe benzo for individuals weaning off alcohol dependence/addiction.

While there have been no studies, to my knowledge, regarding traumatic stress disorder as a result of prolonged benzo withdrawal, I have a strong suspicion that this is an occurring phenomenon.

Additionally, if you are someone that already has post-traumatic stress disorder, and now find yourself going through benzo recovery, your battle is bound to be more challenging. It will be even more important for you to actively engage in your recovery.

Alcohol, Opiates & Benzodiazepines

The problem with dependence is that it often leads to addiction, or at the very least addictive behaviors, such as occasionally taking more meds than needed, or mixing meds with alcohol.

Or perhaps you've got some lower back pain and need to use painkillers for relief, so you sometimes take your benzo and opiate around the same time.

These behaviors are very common for many of us. Things are going to happen, situations will arise, even for the healthiest and most disciplined.

Most of the deaths (and ER visits) in the United States related to benzodiazepine are cases where the drug was mixed with either alcohol or opiates, or both. Respiratory distress, such as labored breathing, is amongst the most common side effect of mixing benzos with alcohol and/or opiates.

If there's one major warning I have for you here, it's to be VERY careful with using alcohol to "take the edge" off your benzo withdrawal symptoms.

As I've stressed already, alcohol has a very similar effect on our brain as a benzo. So, weaning and using alcohol is a lot like weaning and then later taking more benzo, but in a different form, such as titrate.

I've seen more benzo withdrawal failure due to polydrug use, especially with individuals that drink heavily in the evening to alleviate symptoms of withdrawal, than probably anything else—aside from individuals that weaned too quickly and relapsed.

I know the temptation is there to just have a beer (or glass of wine) in the evening, and perhaps one or two will work for you, but also remember that everything is a balancing act and we are all different.

For some people, the slightest bit of alcohol will cause a drastic shift in their taper, resulting in symptom increase.

Of course, the thing you must decide is whether or not the consequences are worth the rewards? Can you find a healthy balance?

Some people can have a couple of drinks in the evening, achieving a little relief from their withdrawal symptoms, and are still able to keep steady and consistent in their weans, with little symptom increase. However, in my experience, alcohol tends to be a problem for most people weaning off benzo. Less is usually more. The same can be said for marijuana.

Marijuana & Benzodiazepine Withdrawal

One question I have received on occasion is whether or not I would recommend marijuana use as a kind of treatment for benzo withdrawal.

I think this is actually a very good question, though one that I understand still carries a taboo.

My thoughts are this— if it works, do it.

We are all looking for relief, and while it can come in different forms, it always seems fleeting. If marijuana gives you some relief, and it doesn't cause you more problems, then why not use it?

Marijuana can be amazing for symptom relief, offering a nice break from the suffering. However, in other people, marijuana instantly triggers anxiety, even panic attacks.

My thoughts on weaning with other drugs, like alcohol or marijuana is that they are typically not ideal. Not only can they exacerbate symptoms, but they still affect the work-reward parts of our brain, the pleasure center of the brain.

The brain is designed so that we feel pleasure for

our work. It drives our human organism to facilitate its survival. When you take a drug, you alter that process, and simply make the brain produce an abundance of "feel-good" chemical reactions regardless of any effort.

When we are weaning off a drug that we have become dependent upon, we have to nurture our recovery. Remember, the brain doesn't really recognize the difference between addiction and dependence. This is why I chose not to take any other chemicals during my own wean.

No alcohol, no marijuana, nothing else.

In fact, I didn't drink alcohol for almost a year after I was completely weaned off benzo. Even then, I drank very little.

Again, if it works, then use it. Just be mindful not to create another problem, as the middle path is a razor's edge.

Therapy, Self-care & Coping Strategies

I use the word therapy, not to suggest any particular theory over another that may be used for treatment, but as a way of framing this next section of the book. Think of these next several chapters as being my attempt at a well-rounded prescription for anyone aiming to recover from benzo dependence.

Most of what I share in this book are techniques taken from cognitive-behavioral psychology. Techniques that deal with how and why our thoughts influence our behavior, and how we can change or alter our thoughts/behavior to achieve better outcomes.

However, this is by no means a sloppy replacement for actual psychotherapy. That said, these techniques worked for many others, myself included.

Self-care and coping strategies are going to be our best friend while facing benzo dependence and withdrawal.

Maintaining a healthy perspective of our condition will play a critical role in recovery. As I have said before, there is no magical pill that will alleviate our benzo symptoms, just as there's no therapy or modality to fix this. The end result, and hopefully our triumph, is the sum of a number of things all combined.

We mustn't think of ourselves as benzo victims. We mustn't become some casualty, injured and sitting on the sideline, waiting for the war to end.

We must decide to actively engage our recovery.

The Ashton Manual & Method

Now we come to one of the more important areas of this book; the weaning process.

There have been a number of excellent books and manuals written and published on benzo tapering, and I encourage you to seek out some of this material. The *Ashton Manual* is perhaps your best resource on tapering currently available, as it has been used successfully by thousands of individuals.

In her manual, Dr. Heather Ashton is very articulate on the topic of benzo tapering and covers much more information that I can here.

That said, I want to paint a picture for you of what the wean process looks like, and what Dr. Ashton's manual advises.

In short, Dr. Ashton's method assists an individual in achieving a slow and steady wean off benzodiazepine by systematically reducing the drug in very small increments each week or two until the drug is entirely out of the system.

Dr. Ashton discovered years ago, through her work with patients addicted to benzo, that withdrawal was sheer hell. During her research, she found that patients who were weaned too quickly experienced significantly more profound negative symptoms and were more likely to relapse after coming off the drug. Eventually, she concluded that patients had much better outcomes if they were able to achieve a slower and smoother taper.

Further, Dr. Ashton's manual recommends that a person consult their physician about switching their benzo to Valium, assuming you weren't already on Valium. The reason for this is that Valium is a long-acting benzo, and it breaks down very slowly in the body, with a half-life of around 200 hours. It's designed for people to take once, maybe twice a day, because it is effective all day and throughout the night.

This is different than short-acting benzos, such as Xanax, which is designed for immediate relief of intense anxiety. However, Xanax leaves the body very quickly, resulting in the need for more frequent dosing.

To give you an idea, the conversion is:

1mg of Xanax = 20 mg of Valium
1mg of Klonopin = 15 mg of Valium
1mg of Ativan = 8 mg of Valium
1mg of Restoril = 0.5 mg of Valium
1mg of Librium = 0.25 mg Valium

Additionally, by switching to Valium, a person has more control over the rate of milligram reduction, as Valium comes in 10mg, 5mg, and 2mg tablets. It also comes in titrate (liquid form). Of course, you should consult your doctor and work with him/her on creating a plan for weaning.

Journal Logs

Keeping a journal log was very helpful for me during my wean because it allowed me to chart my progress, and seeing it in that way was quite inspiring. It's sort of like climbing a mountain and then peeking down at how high you've climbed.

Without a journal log it's easy to lose perspective, and thereby, lose motivation.

Recording your results can also help you to see patterns in your taper, periods where you may notice more or less success. From this data you may be able explain the change in symptoms. Were they related to an increase or decrease in physical activity, or do anxiety symptoms flair up around certain individuals in particular?

One method of journaling is to record our dosing schedule, and perhaps some notes on how we are feeling at the time. These journal entries are sort of our own little doctor's report. If anxiety was particularly high (or low) we might make a note of that. If new symptoms emerge (or old ones disappear), we might record that as well.

Another level of journaling is more personal and intimate. This part is your benzo recovery diary, which can be incredibly therapeutic. It truly is a relief sometimes to just communicate something that's bothering us— even if it's written down, even if we are the only one that will ever read it.

Processing our emotions is part of emotional health.

Journaling also has a way of allowing us to work out our thoughts on paper. It assists us in articulating deeper emotions and thoughts that we otherwise may struggle to fully comprehend, or which are too fearful for us to say out loud.

The Count of Montecristo

I was sitting at my art studio desk, paintbrush in hand, staring at a canvas, feeling completely blank, absolutely uninspired. That's a scary place to be for a professional artist. I began to worry that I'd never feel that creative spark again.

I had made it about half way through my benzo taper at this point.

I'd walk around my room at night and often feel as though I were in some tall castle tower, a kind of suspended prison in the sky. There was no way down, and no one could climb up. I felt as though I were doomed to watch other people live their lives while I wilted away.

One night, I happened to put on a random film, *The Count of Montecristo*. I found myself drawn profoundly to the protagonist of the story, sensing a parallel.

Spoiler alert.

If you recall the story of The Count of Montecristo, it was about a young man unjustly imprisoned in a dungeon for the rest of his life. He spent years chained to a dirty stone wall, and the only light he had came from a tiny opening from which he couldn't even see the outside.

He was without stimulation of any kind.

Each year, on the anniversary of the day he had arrived, the warden would enter his cell and beat his chained body with a whip.

After some years of this torture, when the protagonist was just at the end of his rope, he met an old man that lived in the dungeon next to him. He created a passageway to the old man's cell, and they became close friends.

The old man, who was very wise, offered to teach the protagonist a number of academics, as well as how to sword fight. The young man, who cannot even read or write, accepts this offer. In return, he helps the old man chisel through the thick stone wall in hopes of one day digging to their freedom on the other side.

By the end of the story, the protagonist is finally able to escape the dungeon by using the wit and intellect he had developed through the teachings of the old man. The protagonist then moves to exact revenge on the people who had wronged him. He finds himself reborn, somehow forged into a stronger, more beautiful human being—

though his path to his freedom was nothing short of hell.

He eventually became the Count of Montecristo.

This became hugely inspiring for me because I could deeply relate to the feelings of being imprisoned unjustly, of suffering and of feeling hopeless. I too often felt locked away in some cold grey dungeon, isolated from others, and longing to feel the warmth of the sunlight again.

I looked at the span of my college education up until that point, all that I had accomplished thus far, and I realized all the more what I had been working for and where it could take me.

I realized that I was like the Count of Montecristo, only my old "wise man" were actually men and woman— they were my professors.

That really got me focused and made me work harder.

I also began to look more intensely at my work as an artist. I asked myself if there were things I could be doing to get better, to utilize this time even though I couldn't be creative. Naturally, there were techniques I could learn to advance my skills, and so I did.

The hope that I took with me was that I was going to get better. At the very least, I was working hard to build the kind of future that would be there when I was finally free from benzo hell.

Cognitive-Behavioral Therapy

One of the most valuable things I have learned during my journey to becoming a clinical psychologist has been the effectiveness of cognitive-behavioral therapy for changing behaviors and regulating symptoms.

As I said earlier, it often is not the event in a person's life that creates suffering for the individual, but rather, it is their interpretation, their perception and response to the event that creates the unnecessary suffering in their life.

It's the mental talk that defeats us.

It's the irrational beliefs that take over and start filling in the blanks of our mental and emotional dialogue.

It's the irrational thoughts that tell us we are never going to feel better, that we are weak or that we deserve shame for being in this situation in the first place.

Irrational thinking is negative and misleading self-talk, a byproduct of depression, anxiety, and prolonged stress.

It gets to the best of us, but there are things we can do.

Let's begin with cognitive distortions, or if helps, you can think of them as a kind of unconscious defense mechanisms.

Cognitive distortions (defense mechanisms) are our mind's way of protecting us from thoughts/emotions/perceptions that are too painful or difficult to process. However, it's more complicated than that. These cognitive distortions are amplified by anxiety/stress and are often closely tied to a particular mode of thinking that's being exercised by the individual.

Some argue that these irrational thinking tendencies are wired into our ego, or personality.

These tendencies offer a couple of disservices: they either seek to protect us by blinding us to the truth, thereby giving us rose-colored glasses, OR they do quite the opposite, and the irrational thoughts convince us that we are no good, that we are unloved, and that our condition is hopeless.

It's a complicated mechanism of consciousness, one that spans many theories. Why would our irrational thoughts exist in the first place? Why do they insist on making us miserable?

Well, that depends on which therapist, philosopher, or even scientist, that you ask.

There are a number of identified cognitive distortions.

One that is very common for people experiencing benzo withdrawal is **catastrophizing**. Catastrophizing means that you exaggerate the severity of a situation and instantly jump to the worst-case scenario. It's the great, "what if", that finds its way into over-analyzing each new symptom or bump in the road, not to mention the entire situation as a whole.

Catastrophizing is probably inevitable for you if you're experiencing benzo withdrawal. Your anxiety is through the roof, you're stressed, emotional, worried, and sick and tired of being sick and tired.

I know. It's hell. But it will pass. Deep Breaths

Let's not give in to catastrophizing. Do not drive yourself crazy and create so much unnecessary pain by incessantly asking, "Will I ever get better?"

And never tell yourself, "I will never get better."

You don't know that it isn't going to get better, and by most accounts from people in your situation, they got better. You too will get better.

Now, allow me to bring this point back home.

Cognitive-behavioral therapy can be very useful because it helps us to identify irrational thinking, cognitive distortions, and faulty beliefs. It can aid us in doing things that will help with symptoms, and potentially provide some relief.

Mindfulness meditation and **relaxation** are two techniques that worked wonders for me, and for many others.

Another area that cognitive-behavioral therapists and behavioral therapists will use in treatment for severe anxiety disorders, as well as obsessive-compulsive disorders, is **desensitization**.

Let's take a closer look at these techniques.

Mindfulness

During my early 20's, I struggled with depression and anxiety, particularly after the death of a close family member, and the end of an intensely meaningful romantic relationship. I could sense that I was in trouble, but I didn't want to take meds and I couldn't afford therapy because, at the time, I was but an underpaid cook with no insurance.

This is when I discovered Zen meditation.

At first, I had no idea what it was. I hadn't researched the topic. All I knew was that it focused on sitting in stillness and disconnecting from our incessant, rambling thoughts.

That was a good enough starting point for me. I had a keen instinct not to over analyze the process and was willing to at least try sitting in stillness, disconnecting from my thoughts, and see what (if anything) happened.

My attitude was: this is either works or it doesn't, but I'm not going to join a monastery just to find out.

I began meditating in my own back yard. I would sit there, staring at the line of trees across the field that was swaying to its own rhythm. I decided that every time I came out to this spot for meditation I would try my best to take a break from my daily thoughts and worries.

Sometimes we must give ourselves permission to take a break from our worries, as strange as it may sound.

I would sit there, comfortably if possible, and watch the trees and sky.

At first, my mind would not ease up. In fact, the more I tried to quiet my thoughts, the worst it seemed to get. It was very discouraging, and I began to think that maybe this wasn't for me. Nonetheless, I continued to explore it.

Eventually, realized that it was far easier to tame my mind if I simply stopped trying to do so forcibly. Instead, I would just watch my thoughts as they crept in, as if they were only clouds passing in the sky. The better I got at this; the less active and persistent my thoughts became.

Largely, the reason meditation worked for me was because I entered into the experience with an open mind, and I focused on simply allowing. I allowed my thoughts, but I watched them. I allowed myself some time to simply put aside my worries, even the big ones, the ones that I convinced myself that I needed to be focusing on 25 hours a day or else my life would fall apart.

I put those aside too, if for only 20 minutes a day.

Almost immediately I felt an effect. Firstly, my anxiety and depression symptoms were fading quickly. My thoughts seemed lighter, freer, and less intrusive. I had never experienced anything like this before in my life. The most fascinating part to me was that this experience seemed to be growing.

What had begun as a flicker of peace soon became something much more. I got the very real sense that there were perhaps deeper levels that could be attained.

The more I meditated, the better I felt. The more my thoughts calmed down, I could choose when to use my mind, rather than being a spectator of the incessant thought-marathon inside my head. Additionally, my mind was sharper and able to focus better. Things I read and heard, I retained better than I had ever before.

At this point, I decided to go back and really study Zen meditation. This turned me on to a number of Eastern meditative practices, such as Yoga, Daoism, Sufism, and Buddhism.

Before someone asks, Zen is essentially Buddhism minus any explanation, interpretation, exaggeration, or dogma. One should begin with Zen, not Buddhism as a religion or system of philosophy. If you begin with Zen, then you will likely find that Buddhism explains a lot of what you're experiencing.

If you begin with Buddhism, then it's like having someone explain in great detail the special place to which you're planning a vacation but have never been before. You can do that, or you can simply go and see for yourself.

This was a big part of my thinking, and I feel it is worth noting. Zen is the method. Buddhism is the explanation. However, the method will get you to the same spaces of consciousness.

That said, the more I read on Zen, the more it resonated with me.

Needless to say, it had a profound impact on my mental health. Not only did it ward off symptoms of depression, anxiety and stress, but it also promoted healthier states of consciousness, and much more emotional regulation.

Further, my personality became somehow more authentic, and I was less tensed, negative, and reactive to the various problematic situations. I can honestly say that the practice of Zen meditation positively enhanced virtually every aspect of my life.

Even my artistic work improved.

I knew then that there was something more to this, and I wondered if psychology and science were aware of the effects of meditation, or did they just view it as some kind pseudo spiritual placebo?

What I discovered was, yes, science and psychology both were aware of these positive effects. In fact, a wealth of research has been done on the effects of meditation and mindfulness on anxiety, depression, personality disorders, and traumatic-stress.

Moreover, psychology had long been implementing techniques learned from Zen meditation in treatment of mental health.

A lot of what we see in cognitive-behavioral therapy, and especially dialectical-behavioral therapy, are principles grounded in Zen meditation. Practices such as self-awareness through entering the present moment and learning to accept the current moment as it is, without feeling compelled to force change.

If you can learn to meditate during your recovery, you may experience profound relief. However, it is also worth noting that during the beginning of my taper I did find it very difficult to meditate. Perhaps my symptoms were too severe at this point, because whenever I attempted to stop my mind, it only seemed to amplify.

This is partially due to the nature of our mind, and the reason why meditation instructors tell us to allow the thoughts, without attempting to force their removal. Observing them without getting emotionally involved is enough.

Later in my taper, meditation became essential, and I used mindfulness to relax and alleviate the incessant chatter in my head. It helped me tremendously to identify faulty thinking patterns, self-defeating perceptions, and to gently ease those distortions back to sleep.

For more information on Zen I recommend reading books on this subject from Alan Watts, a Westerner that spent much time in the East learning Buddhism. He provides a wonderful and simple teaching on Zen and meditation.

Breathing

One of the most common symptoms of anxiety is difficulty breathing, which is why we often hyperventilate when having a panic attack. When we hyperventilate we breathe faster than normal, and we tend to exhale more than we inhale. This disrupts the healthy balances of breathing in air and exhaling carbon dioxide.

Additionally, this difficulty breathing often triggers more panic responses, because we feel as though we are suffocating. We may even become light-headed, or feint. Panic attacks are severely frightening.

One of the best things that you can do when you feel a jolt of anxiety, especially a jolt that instantly gets your heart rate up, is to immediately focus on calming yourself. Slow your breathing, inhaling and exhaling equally.

Breathe in through your nose for a slow 2 or 3 count, and then exhale from your mouth for a slow 2 or 3 count. Repeat this for 2 minutes. At the same time, try to relax. As difficult as that is, we get better at beating panic by responding to its alarms with a sense of ease, grace, and courage.

Further, breathing promotes positive health, and can have a huge impact on reducing stress and anxiety.

It all begins with breathing.

Do not worry about your thoughts, just focus on your breath. Let that be your meditation or mantra.

We can and should practice controlled breathing throughout our day, for just a couple of minutes here and there.

One good exercise is learning to access our diaphragm during breathing. Vocalists are taught the same technique; singing from their diaphragm rather than the throat. The difference is huge, btw.

Picture your diaphragm as being a small balloon in the center of your abdomen, just below your heart, or in the stomach in region.

As you inhale slowly through your nose, you imagine yourself blowing up the balloon. When it's nice and filled, you pause for a moment, then exhale slowly through your mouth, feeling the air escaping the balloon (diaphragm).

You will be able to feel a slight contraction in your diaphragm, especially as you exhale.

This takes practice, and after some time it becomes much more effortless. With practice you will strengthen your ability to control your breathing, to slow it down, and with it, your heart rate, and racing thoughts.

You will know your meditative breathing is working when you begin to feel your heart rate slowing down, or when you begin yawning.

If the only thing you achieve in mastering this breathing exercise is that it bores you to sleep, then take it, because sleep is a luxury when you're coming off benzodiazepines.

Desensitization, Exposure Therapy & Panic Attack

Anxiety cannot coexist with relaxation.

If you can manage to relax, you will see your anxiety plummet. The problem will be achieving this state of relaxation while suffering anxiety. What a paradox.

It is true, anxiety is a goliath wall that we must face. It is a monumental challenge, but we *can* eventually get to the other side by systematically chipping away at the stone. It is only with daily effort, over time, that you really begin to see behavioral techniques start to work.

One such technique that we can use is Systematic Desensitization. With this method, a person first achieves relaxation, and then slowly begins to mentally/emotionally explore fearful ideas until those ideas are no longer perceived as a danger.

It's kind of like easing your body into a really hot bath. We begin by dipping our toes into the water, then our foot, then our leg…

For example, if you happen to be afraid of driving over bridges, having experienced a panic attack as result of driving over bridges, then you could use systematic desensitization to gradually reduce your brain's fight or flight response to this stimulus.

Systematic desensitization begins with small fear stimuli, and gradually progresses into more profound fear stimuli.

Fear is much less overwhelming when we break it down into its basic parts.

Eventually, our brain, which, behaviorally speaking is rather lazy, will stop working so hard to activate our fight or flight response. It's too taxing on the body and the brain isn't getting anything out of it. The only time the brain benefits by triggering a fight or flight response is when that survival response keeps us out of danger.

We can appreciate the brain jolting us with adrenaline and hyper vigilance, when we need to escape a predator, or survive an accident. However, when there is no predator or imminent danger, it is simply unnecessary and self-harming.

A panic attack is exactly that— a survival mechanism in the body that has gotten its wires crossed, randomly activating due to misinterpreted signals. Think of it like a smoke detector that is malfunctioning and keeps randomly going off.

Benzo withdrawal is a combination of biological responses and mental processes. And like the faulty smoke detector, these biological responses randomly sound alarms in our mind, triggering anxiety and panic, as a result of misinterpreted signals. This is where desensitization methods come in, working to rewire our thinking process.

Walking to the mailbox daily is one approach to desensitization if, for example, you have agoraphobia. We call this **exposure**, and there is an entire therapy based on it.

Another example would be going out to eat daily at a semi-busy cafeteria on your lunch break as a kind of desensitization (exposure), if you have social anxiety.

While this may be uncomfortable, our minds eventually adapt and reduce anxious signals. Over time, we come to realize that there is no actual danger while we are having lunch in a room full of other people.

As you can see, exposure therapy is a more 'hands on' extreme version of desensitization. With desensitization therapy the person is allowed to sit safely at home and imagine fearful stimulus. However, exposure therapy requires you to face real situations and places as we take the next step and engage the fear.

Remember this, although it's hard to believe at times going through severe withdrawal, but our body does want us to survive.

Our organism was designed by nature over billions of years to adapt and survive. And if survival means being able to be around busy crowds when you have anxiety, eventually the body *will* adapt, and the anxiety will reduce.

Survival > Irrational fears = Nature's Math

Exposure therapy relies on our body's ability to adapt to fearful stimulus that has been revealed as false, thereby reducing anxiety and stress responses.

When you show the brain that its panic responses are unnecessary and counterproductive to survival, it tends to relax.

Now, real fearful stimulus is another story.

If you were being chased by a grizzly bear, I doubt any amount of exposure is going to result in a reduction of anxiety. Though it is worth noting that as a human being it is possible to become quite desensitized to even some of the most intense and unbelievable traumatic situations.

One of the best things that I did for my anxiety was to expose myself to fear. I beat social anxiety by forcing myself to be in social situations, and I beat panic disorder by learning how to be comfortable in uncomfortable situations—by showing my brain that it was okay to relax, that I was safe, and that these panic signals were unnecessary.

It took some time, and a lot of practice, but it worked. I will expand more on this topic later.

Pet Therapy

I want to say a quick word about the therapeutic value of having a loving pet around while we are going through tough withdrawals. During my own experiences, I had my hybrid wolf dog (Gambit) at my side daily. We bonded incredibly during that time and in his own way he was wonderfully sympathetic to my condition. He woke me up each morning with his big bright eyes, and he sort of nudged me out of bed. As if he were saying, "Come on, Dave, let's go!"

It was a nice way to wake up each morning. And when I couldn't sleep, he would lay with me and keep me company throughout the night.

Having a furry companion can really help with symptoms, reducing some of the anxiety, giving us something to care for and look after. And this is more than just my own opinion; a number of scientific studies have shown the positive affect that pets can have on a person's anxiety, depression, and emotional support. Even a fish tank can be surprisingly comforting.

Having a pet is a minor responsibility that will help you to get out of bed in the morning, up and moving. If you don't already have a pet, and can perhaps adopt one, I'd encourage that during this challenging process.

Distractions

The best distraction is the one that works.

The next best distraction is the one that offers us something in return, such as an increase in our skills, knowledge, abilities, or awareness.

For me, college was a great distraction from my condition, as it forced me to focus on things other than my terrible disposition. Additionally, it gave me something positive to work for, and it gave me hope for the future.

Now, depending on where you are in your benzo recovery, something as demanding as college may not be realistic. However, they do offer online classes, which can allow us the comfort of staying up and working on our studies at our own pace, in our own home. You might also consider some sort of educational focus on a smaller scale, such as; workshops, clubs, studio memberships, classroom auditing etc.

In all honesty, it's not going to be easy either way. None of your typical distractions or old hobbies are going to come as easy as they once did. Especially the ones that drive us further outside of our comfort zones, such as going to a college campus for night classes or driving to a public park to go for walks where there are other people.

The engagement of these activities will be difficult at first. They're going to be challenging. Even gardening in our own backyard will be hard for us in the beginning, but we must push forward. It is in part this ability to engage, despite our fears and the challenges, that will foster a huge aspect of our recovery.

Taking up hobbies may be difficult, but it can also be hugely distracting, therapeutic, and rewarding. Gardening, fishing, reading, building/creating things, or perhaps taking on small doable projects around the house when you feel up to it, all can offer us a momentary break from the benzo hurricane going on in our head and body.

Pushing forward, despite our fears, is one of the boldest spices in our healing recipe. And it's the only way out.

Setting Goals:
The Foundation for Success

Setting goals can be the key to success in many areas of our life, from dieting and losing weight, to reaching new accomplishments in our work, career, education, or sport. With benzo recovery, setting goals is essential.

Everything you're doing for your wean comes down to setting goals and micromanaging. You're constantly planning out your days, weeks, months, setting goals, i.e., "by next month I will have reduced 1-2+ milligrams from my daily dose" Or, "by this time next year, I want to be completely off the meds and going for daily walks around the block."

The better organized that we can make things for ourselves, the easier it will be.

Every two weeks I would set new goals. I was gentle with myself, and yet disciplined. I expected to meet my goals, but I didn't beat myself up if I had a tougher week and had to go slower. Other goals were motivational, such as being more active around the house, or finishing up various projects. I recorded my goals in a journal as a reminder and for general record keeping of my progress.

Lifestyle Change
(you must work)

This is a good topic that bridges all of the things I have discussed so far with all the things I have to say from here out. Lifestyle change is going to be key during your wean and is likely to be even more important after your last dose of benzo (or any drug for that matter).

The reason why most disciplines fail, i.e., dieting, exercising, etc., is because we attempt to do too much too quickly.

I always tell people that if you want to change your diet to be healthier, then start by removing one item that's unhealthy. Don't immediately jump to removing all the bad stuff while introducing a ton of food that you've previously avoided because you don't really like it.

This is a sure way to fail.

The same can be said with physical fitness. Let's be honest, most of us do not exercise. Then, one day, usually after some kind of epiphany, we decide that we are going to start a workout routine. We join a gym, or purchase exercise equipment. We try to learn various exercises, focusing on all of the muscle groups; training legs on a certain day, and arms, back, and chest on others.

And it all quickly becomes overwhelming. It is simply too much too soon.

Start small.

Begin by going for short walks and doing light stretches. Maybe get a pair of light dumbbells and do basic simple exercises, such as bicep curls.

We start light, but we stay consistent. Small steps lead to giant strides.

Eventually it becomes part of our lifestyle, just as our diet becomes part of our lifestyle, and that is when real long-lasting change takes place.

Getting free from benzo hell requires a lot from us, physically, mentally, emotionally, and even spiritually.

Laying down and just waiting for it to pass is the worst thing we can do. Most failed cases, where people really struggle after coming off benzo, are with the individuals that crawled into bed for several months. They developed unhealthy habits, and their depression and anxiety skyrocketed.

It even happened to me for a period of time.

It's a tough fight, no doubt. The anxiety, stress, depression, and a whole host of other benzo symptoms inevitably kick our butts. We get overcome with fatigue, and we just crawl into bed. I didn't know any better then, but I do now, and I am going to strongly emphasize this point to you.

Lifestyle changes are **key.**

What do I mean by lifestyle changes exactly?

I'm talking about taking care of ourselves and doing what we need to do daily so that we stay healthy and balanced. Which, in turn, will hopefully help in battling our ever-growing forest of anxieties while we wait out this benzo storm.

We can focus on things like our hygiene, being more active around the house, healthier eating, getting enough water, getting enough sleep (even if you have to steal a few hours here and there), interacting with friends and family (even if only on social media). We can also lean on support groups for help, hope and information.

We should exercise daily, even if it means only walking to the mailbox and back, to the stop sign and back, or around the block and back, and so on.

I realize "lifestyle change" may seem a little obvious. Perhaps even inevitable, but I want to remind you of the nature of the beast that is benzo withdrawal. It is a multi-headed serpent: one head is depression, one head is stress, one head is anxiety, and the other heads are a host of other physical and mental symptoms.

All these things can have a seriously debilitating effect on us. Depression alone can render us completely disabled. The advice I give here is designed to battle all the heads that you will face, because the first thing that this beast takes from us is our lifestyle.

Think of lifestyle change as constructing a system of checks and balances, to make sure we are striving to be healthy despite our disposition.

Any positive step forward is a positive step worth making.

The point I want to end this topic on is the value of sheer effort.

I cannot say this enough. You cannot lie down and let benzo take over your life. You must get up, you must strive to be active and engaged, to find meaning and hope within your life.

If this were an old action film from the 1980's (which I am very fond of btw), this would be the point in the film where you've suffered a major setback but are more determined than ever to overcome. So, you go away for a bit and begin training hard for the final battle.

Think of this period as your montage.

Religion, Spirituality & Withdrawal

Religion and spirituality can be an incredibly powerful support system for anyone undergoing an intense struggle in their life. In fact, all metaphysical notions aside, studies have shown positive correlations between prayer/spirituality, and a person's health, both physically and mentally. The scientific explanation for this is that these practices have a very psychotherapeutic meditative affect upon the individual. In addition, it also gives them hope and something to strive for and believe in.

Quite simply— when things get too heavy, we can ask God or a higher power to take some of that burden from us. For some, this may be quite powerful.

This may or may not work for you, depending on your religious or spiritual background.

As I said before, *If it helps, do it*. If church or a monastery can be a support group, use it.

Perhaps you're not religious, but you're spiritual. Maybe you meditate, simply celebrating goodness and love. Great. Use it. Confide in love. Confide in goodness. Goodness feels good, right? Allow your spirituality to help guide you and, ease some of your pain.

Perhaps you're neither religious nor spiritual, but you do have a keen eye for what's really important in this life. You know how to celebrate that importance, and you know how to feel deeply, to love deeply, and to strive for peace. Great. Use it.

So much of our suffering is either created, or in some way amplified, by our thoughts, feelings, beliefs, irrationality, and then reinforced through our behaviors. Often, it is not the event itself that hurts us the most, but rather our misinterpretation of the event.

Religion, spirituality, or what you could simply think of as a solid moral and humanistic core, can be powerfully healing.

And remember this, having a religious or spiritual or humanistic base means having faith in the truest sense, and by that, I mean, having faith that things will work out.

Our religion or spirituality should lift us up and help us to become better human beings, better versions of ourselves.

It can be our lighthouse on the darkest nights of our existence.

Common Core Health:
Sleep, Diet, & Exercise

In all that I have learned about health, both physical and mental, three fundamental elements of life have worked their way into my everyday prescription. Sleep. Diet. Exercise.

Sleep, diet, and exercise, are huge chunks in the pie of health, physically, mentally, and emotionally speaking.

This is particularly true when you have anxiety/depression, are undergoing intense prolonged stress, and are weaning off benzo dependence. During benzo recovery our body goes through a traumatic and dynamic process of withdrawal and re-regulation, as our nervous system struggles to regain balance.

When we do not get enough sleep (7-9 hours each day) a number of negative symptoms quickly emerge. To begin with, our anxiety goes way up, our ability to fight stress goes way down, we become more vulnerable to depression, our memory and cognitive abilities decrease significantly, our moods alter, and we can become more aggressive. And this happens after only a few days of not getting enough sleep.

Studies have shown that people who only getting 6 hours of sleep each night, after a period of several consecutive nights, produced cognitive performances similar to that of an individual that hasn't slept in 24 hours. Individuals that only got 4 hours of sleep a night had increasingly drastic declines in cognitive performance, which worsened each day.

When it gets to the point of weeks and months without the quality of sleep that we need, (not staying asleep long enough or deep enough to reach those life replenishing brain waves) these conditions become greatly amplified.

Furthermore, lack of sleep has a profound impact on our perception and can even lead to delusion and psychosis.

The problem with benzo withdrawal is that the medication that had once helped you to sleep, is now robbing you of the rest you need. Still, we find sleep where we can. Sometimes all we get are catnaps, but we also need to make time for full, uninterrupted rest. Sleep does not work like a bank account where the naps add up to meet a quota. You need a full night's sleep to properly replenish and rejuvenate, both mentally and physically.

Again, sounds too obvious, right? "Make time for sleep? DUH!"

Fair enough, but we can easily slip into that obsessive worrying cycle that gets those stress hormones pumping, which in return tend to hinder our ability to sleep. Incessant worrying kept me up more nights than I can remember during my taper.

The biological disposition is always there with benzo withdrawal, always screwing with our chemistry, and always creating symptoms such as anxiety.

The thing I have tried to emphasize in this chapter is the understanding that our biology and thoughts are closely interconnected, and they feed one another. The more benzo messes with our chemistry, the more stress and anxiety we experience, and after prolonged stress and anxiety, our perception begins to change.

We worry more, and this triggers more anxiety and stress in our body. It becomes a disruptive, potentially debilitating, cycle.

Another point worth mentioning is that a lack of sleep is also correlated with an increase in pain sensitivity. Naturally, when you're going through benzo withdrawal symptoms pain sensitivity is one of the last things you want.

When I was weaning off benzo, I was also dealing with some wretched lower back issues, which stemmed from another car accident I'd had as a teenager. I instantly noticed a correlation between a lack of sleep and an increase in pain sensitivity. In fact, it almost got away from me, as I began to psychologically amplify the pain through catastrophizing the pain signals. Essentially, taking a pain level of 4 to an 8, and creating a ton of unnecessary additional anxiety for myself.

Now that we've discussed the negative effects of benzo insomnia you may be wondering what you can do to achieve sleep. To that million-dollar question I regretfully inform you that there is not much one *can* do, at least not anything that will provide immediate relief. Yes, there are sleeping aids, but the trouble with that is their dangerous similarity to a benzo and how quickly they can create more negative symptoms for you. If you should decide to take a sleeping aid I suggest that you do so with caution, being very aware of any increase or change in symptoms.

As I've said before, everyone experiences benzo withdrawal differently. I've known people who took sleeping aids during the tapering process and didn't seem to have any problem at all. Alternatively, I've witnessed a number of cases where the sleeping aid created more problems than it solved.

The best advice I can give regarding sleep is to remember that our body is an organism of adaptation. We begin by carving out a meditative hour or so each day, typically just before you would fall asleep is ideal. We must create a sleep habit and ritual for ourselves.

Remember to strive for good *sleep hygiene,* which involves cleaning up our sleep routine, freeing our sleep space of electronics, and other distractions. This means turning off our TVs and phones at least an hour before bed, and removing lights in the room, as certain light can mess with our natural circadian clock.

I was fortunate to have an old hot tub at my house and in the evenings, I would sit in it and try to clear my mind. I'd purposely focus on allowing my skin and muscles to feel the warmth of the water, imagining each jet massaging away my aches and tension. It was very visual for me. At first, it wasn't easy to get comfortable. In fact, it was damn near impossible, but I confided in the principle of classical conditioning.

I knew that if I really put effort into it and could

find even the briefest moment of relaxation, or pleasure that I could work with that moment and make it grow into something more therapeutic.

In essence, the hot tub became my relaxation meditation therapy tank. I even found ways to further improve my experience by adding pleasant fragrances to the water, especially lavender and vanilla.

When I couldn't be in the hot tub, I found that a hot shower or bath was a great alternative. Each time, I would make a conscious effort to take a break from my thoughts while I was in the water. I considered this my Zen water therapy.

As silly as it may sound, this is precisely what we must do! We must make a conscious decision to take a break from the worrying. We must give ourselves permission, saying, "okay, I'm going to take an hour break and then we can jump back into the mathematical loop that has no answer."

After a couple of weeks, and even more so after a couple of months, I really began to experience true moments of relief. They may have been brief moments, but that can go a long way when tapering from benzo. I am sharing this with you because not only did I get symptom relief, but it also relaxed me enough so that I had a better shot at falling and staying asleep when I needed to.

Additionally, as I began to experience new levels of relief from these relaxation techniques, I started to get more creative in the endeavor. I installed special ambient lighting for my bedroom and would play atmospheric music to sleep to. Sometimes I'd listen to sounds of the ocean, other times I'd listen to an old Alan Watts lecture, enjoying the tranquilizing effect of his voice.

I did my best to avoid caffeine and if I did partake, then I made sure it was several hours before I'd hope to fall asleep. Staying away from caffeine wasn't too hard though, considering that this seemingly harmless substance *increased* my anxiety symptoms. And when I *did* crave the relaxation of a warm beverage, I would instead make myself a nice cup of chamomile tea before bed, often in my hot tub or bathtub, as it has quite a relaxing effect.

Successful sleep, for me, meant sticking to a bedtime routine: hot tub, bath, maybe some light stretching and meditative breathing, soft music, hot tea, maybe some candlelight and pleasant-smelling lotion, or incense.

A bit of light reading before bed also helped. Note, I said *light reading*, as I would not advise reading a thriller or horror novel before bed.

And If my mind was being overactive, as it usually was, I wouldn't fight my thoughts. Instead, I'd just get up and play cards or engage in some other kind of mental activity that allowed my mind to run a few mental laps.

Everything about successful benzo recovery will come down to a balancing act of maintaining healthy routines, even when we don't feel like it or don't see the immediate results.

Final note on sleep— there are a few supplements you might explore that may help you into a more restful night, such as valerian root and melatonin. And before you ask, or before someone falsely informs you, valerian root is <u>not</u> what Valium is made from. I do not know how or where that belief got started, but I have heard it many times.

Valerian root is completely natural and can be purchased from many grocery or health food stores. It is most commonly used to treat insomnia, but it also has an anxiety reducing quality and can help alleviate symptoms of depression as well. Additionally, valerian root is used to treat muscle and joint pain.

Melatonin is also available at most grocery or health stores. It is a supplement based on a hormone found naturally in the body that can be very helpful in promoting sleep. Many people use melatonin for jet lag, but it can also be helpful for insomnia. The most common side effect is vivid and/or bizarre dreams.

I've have not found there to be any negative reports on side effects for valerian root; however, its beneficial qualities haven't been effective in every case. The same thing can be said of melatonin. The effect is different for each individual.

Diet

It is vitally important that we eat a well-balanced selection of food each day. Think on the *color wheel of food*, and make sure that you have something from each color on your plate, i.e., greens, carrots, and tomatoes. In addition to eating well, you'll also want to drink plenty of water, three bottles or more a day.

In addition, you'll want to be mindful that certain foods are going to cause you more anxiety and stress, thus should be carefully considered during a benzo taper.

Digest too many sugars, carbs, or caffeine, and you're basically asking for an increase in anxiety, if not a full-blown panic attack. Many people completely cut these things out of their diet while they are weaning. It's also just a smarter, healthier choice overall, no matter your mental state.

When I was going through my withdrawal I ate fish regularly, particularly baked salmon with extra lemon and garlic. This was a great source of omega 3 fatty acids, which have a ton of health benefits. To begin with, the omega 3's in fish have been proved to lower elevated triglyceride levels, resulting in a decrease in heart disease. They can also help with stiffness and joint pain associated with rheumatoid arthritis and have been shown to have a positive effect in cases of depression.

And, considering that depression and anxiety are two sides of the same coin, depression relief results in anxiety relief.

Alternately, if you don't like fish, or simply do not eat enough of it, you can always get your omega 3 in flaxseed, canola oil, and soybean oil, as well as omega 3 supplements, such as fish oil. Personally, I like to eat walnuts daily, which are a great source of omega 3.

Exercise

Finally, we come to exercise.

Nothing is perhaps healthier for benzo recovery than physical activity. Regular exercise has incredible health benefits, not only resulting in weight loss and cardiovascular health, but also in promoting mental health.

Exercise has been shown in many studies to have a direct positive effect on mood, relaxation, pleasure, and sleep. It can also greatly reduce symptoms of anxiety, stress and depression, which can help to regulate a better quality of sleep.

Exercise can be extremely therapeutic during our recovery, if we allow it and if we work for it.

And we *do* have to work for it—and work hard.

Even more so, as we are currently dealing with the fatigue that comes with benzo tapering. I mean, how does one exercise with such intense fatigue? Not to mention, I'm not getting enough sleep, and my anxiety is through the roof.

We meet the challenge gradually. That's how.

The name of the game is "baby steps," just like that film with Bill Murray. We take small steps at first and we build off them, consistently. Lack of consistence is the number one reason behavioral therapies fail when treating illnesses like anxiety, panic attack, and depression. The symptoms beat us down and we submit.

We cannot allow this.

Also, worth noting, lack of consistency is the number one reason exercise and diet programs fail as well.

If we can accomplish just 10-30 minutes of light cardio a day then we are doing something positive to ensure our recovery.

If you can work up to weight training, I mean really getting a sweat going and getting those muscles pumped, then you will experience even better results.

To drive this section home, I want to reiterate the importance of a *lifestyle change* when recovering from benzo dependence.

Routines become habits, and habits become lifestyles.

Sunlight & Vitamin D

Often is the case that we find ourselves inside the house far too much during our benzo taper, and even long after our last dose. This is particularly true for agoraphobics and others with intense anxiety. While staying inside too much may seem harmless outside the lack of social interaction, it actually contributes negatively to our withdrawal symptoms.

Our body is designed by nature to absorb sunlight and convert it into vitamin D. And we need vitamin D, as it serves several functions in the body. Some of these functions include; promoting bone growth and density. Whereas the lack of vitamin D has been linked to breast, colon and prostate cancers, heart disease, weight gain and depression.

Spending too much time inside, not getting enough vitamin D, can create or aggravate existing depression. Seasonal Affective Disorder (SAD) is a type of depression that's related to changes in the season associated with prolonged periods of inefficient light conditions. SAD is common in places like Alaska where there is extended periods of near darkness.

So, make sure that you're getting enough sunlight on a daily basis. Alternately, if you can't get enough sunlight then you can eat foods high in vitamin D, such as salmon, tuna, egg yolk, or fortified cereals. You can also get vitamin D in milk, and in some orange juice, or you can take vitamin D supplements.

Fishing therapy

This may perhaps be a strange topic for a book like this, but fishing helped me so much during my recovery, in at least a few incredible ways.

Firstly, it got me out of the house, an amazing feat in itself. And not only did I leave the house, but I had to travel in order to get to the lake, unload my little boat, then push away from shore and troll out into the water.

Everyone else on the boat was having a great time, enjoying every moment— all, except me. For me, it was nothing short of exposure therapy, at least initially. It was like a full-day exercise in fighting off a panic attack.

The thing that scared me the most was the feeling of helplessness as we moved further and further away from the shore. It literally set off alarms in my head. I had terrific anxiety.

However, at the same time, I also loved fishing and had always found pleasure it. I knew that if I could get past the fear and anxiety symptoms that I might catch a few brief moments of the joy I've always had while fishing.

Those fleeting moments of joy *did* come. Sometimes with a nice catch, other times with a picturesque sunset.

The moments were small at first, in contrast to the symptoms that were so strong and fierce. But, after some months, I did begin to adapt. Anxiety diminished. Panic diminished, and eventually both went away for the most part while I was out there on the water. I still had anxiety because of what I was going through, but it was no longer setting off fire alarms in head.

This example illustrates a behavioral therapeutic point that I have been sharing in various forms throughout this book; that safe exposure to irrational fear will eventually lead to diminished irrational responses.

We can accomplish this by confronting our fears while also finding a way to be comfortable, such as fishing, gardening, yoga, or meditating in a hot tub.

Positive Attitude & Visualization

They say a positive attitude goes a long way, and it really does. Medical doctors and mental health professionals recognize this all the time. Attitude is directly related to emotional burnout and stress response.

How we view the world shapes our world.

And while we'd like to think that for the most part our perception is fairly accurate, the truth is, when we are under stress we begin to see the world in a profoundly different way. Prolonged stress results in hyper vigilance, irritability, negativity, anxiety, and even depression.

This quickly and almost inevitably develops a loop, a continuous self-feeding loop of manifesting symptoms.

When we do find ourselves lost in these negative/anxious/depressive loops, we must work to break free and see reality clearly again. It may seem minor, even trivial, but it starts with small changes in how you see things, events, and people, and in how you interact with these things.

Suddenly, you're suspicious that a coworker is judging you when, most likely, they weren't even thinking about you. Your spouse answers you a little too loudly and you become upset, because in your eyes they just freaked out on you, when in fact they hadn't.

These are small changes in how we interpret our environment, but they can have huge implications, and if left unattended they will run wild and manifest into worst things.

We've spoken a lot already on negative self-defeating talk. Positive attitude is the exact opposite of that. We must punch through the fabric of negativity, so we can realign with ourselves— and this must become a daily ritual. It's a ritual of spotting the lie, and then putting it down.

Here's the thing.

You're either going to get better or you're not.

Or, you're going to get a little better, then you're going to level off.

These are your basic outcomes. However, I am telling you, so you can inform yourself, that most people get better and recover from benzo withdrawal.

That's a fact. Confide in that fact.

It is far more likely that you're going to be one of the 95% that get better, than it is to assume you are part of the 5% that may continue to struggle.

And when we look at the rarest cases, the ones with people who are still having symptoms 3+ years after withdrawal, we see strong correlations with other variables, such as: how long they took the drug, their abuse of other drugs at the same time, their continued abuse of other drugs, other medical conditions that might account for their symptoms, other psychotropic meds that might be creating their symptoms or prolonging their condition. In addition, we might ask, are they actively trying to get better, or did they surrender to the symptoms (or were simply overcome by the symptoms) to the point that other illnesses have now developed?

Bottom line. People *do* recover from benzo withdrawal. There *is* life after benzo. However, as I've said a number of times in this book, you will greatly facilitate your recovery if you can actively work at doing the things you need to do to promote your recovery. This typically means a lot of hard work and putting yourself in uncomfortable positions. Do it. It will pay off tremendously in the end.

If you take nothing else away with you from this book, please take some peace of mind, some faith, and some hope in your recovery. Keep your attitude positive; focus on the dosages and all the progress you're making. Keep a journal to record your progress.

Set weekly goals and be proud as you reach those goals.

Believe in your strength. Believe in your heart. Start planning your release from the benzo prison cell and allow yourself to daydream about all of the possible future paths ahead of you.

Stay positive. Trust in your recovery. I know it's dark and it can seem hopeless but always remember, you are going to get better.

Here's another way of looking at it. Worrying and believing that you're not going to get better does absolutely nothing to help your condition, and in fact, only makes you suffer more.

The physical symptoms are hell, but the mental anguish and mental pain can be far more traumatic.

Positive attitude can get us through unbelievably difficult times. Use it like a vitamin.

And remember. You can have symptoms, but you don't have to identify with them. You don't have to allow your condition to beat down your ability to keep the faith in your recovery.

Support Groups:
Family, Friends & Forums

Fortunately for us today, opposed to even 20-30 years ago, we have an abundance of resources at our fingertips. We can find information online in a matter of minutes that can greatly serve us in our recovery. We can hear stories from real people with similar experiences through various YouTube channels dedicated to bringing exposure to benzo withdrawal.

Support groups are essential to recovery for anyone dealing with addiction. I found a lot of comfort (and some fear) in a few benzo support group forums that I found online. If you would like to explore this option, and I highly recommend that you do, simply type "Benzodiazepine Withdrawal Support Forums" into the Google search engine

Two of the more frequented benzo forums are:

www.BenzoBuddies.org
www.Benzosupport.org

A quick reminder and word of caution. Do not be overwhelmed by the number of negative stories you will undoubtedly hear. These are rare cases and are not true reflections of the entire population going through benzo withdrawal.

The problem is, most people (after they get better) are eager to get back to living. Once they feel better they don't tend to come back to the support group forums and YouTube videos/comments sections. They might produce a video or two as a follow up that communicates that they're feeling better, but then you often do not hear from them again.

However, what *does* remain are the dozen or so videos they made while going through their withdrawals that show them stuck in hell, and likely feeling hopeless.

The other concern is that you will hear stories of people that are simply going through prolonged hell and don't seem to be recovering. They could be 3 to 4 years off benzo and still experiencing horrible symptoms of anxiety or worse.

These are the stories that will most frighten us, and we think, "Please don't let that be me!" And of course, after some months of constantly stressing and worrying we often think, "That IS going to be me! I just know it!"

Again, you don't know that to be true. Remember, the tragic accounts of people not getting better are perhaps 1% of the entire benzo withdrawal population.

In addition to online forums, and communication with other individuals sharing our hell, we can and should lean a bit on our family and friends.

That's part of the reason we are in each other's lives. To be there for one another, in good times and bad.

Don't be ashamed of your disposition, and don't worry about being a burden. You're wounded, and you need a helping hand. Take it. Accept it. Be grateful.

Besides, if it makes you feel more comfortable, you can set a goal to make it up to them after you're all better.

I was very fortunate at the time of my benzo taper because I had a very good support group. Support groups are huge predictors of outcome for individuals facing recovery.

A strong support group can be the difference between success and failure.

We don not need negative people beating us down over our predicament or expecting too much out of us while we are sick. We need understanding and compassion, and if your friend/family/spouse doesn't understand your situation, then help them to. Share this book with them or let them see the forums and testimonies of others. You most likely will need to do some friendly educating, but that's true with most uncommon conditions.

Having the right people around you can help to carry you through this hell, while surrounding yourself with the wrong people can make climbing this mountain seem impossible.

In the case of truly negative people, those that seem to punish us for being sick, they can actually make our condition far more severe.

The best advice I can offer is that you try to create a support group for yourself, both online and in your personal life.

Explain to them what you're going through and allow them to sympathize and understand some of what you're experiencing.

In my situation, I was fortunate because I had a couple of friends that came around regularly to get me out of the house and engaged in some activity, such as going for walks, exercising, or fishing.

However, the person that probably will be our best friend and our greatest companion while we navigate through benzo hell, is our spouse. It's our wife/girlfriend/boyfriend/husband that we will inevitably lean on the hardest.

God bless these people.

We should try and remember as often as we can that unfortunately we inevitably are a burden to these people at times, but that this is temporary.

Even if it takes some years to fully work out, it is temporary.

The best we can do is to try and not allow our miserable condition, and our miserable symptoms negatively affect our significant other. We have to keep an eye on our moods, and try not to be snappy, irritable, frustrated, or even mean, to our significant other. They're frustrated too. They're concerned and have been worrying sick about you for a long time too.

It's okay. This is the way it is with most serious illnesses or life events. It's okay. What's not okay is treating your significant other like a whipping post for your own frustrations and discontent.

Lean on your support group.

Accept your current disposition.

There's no space for guilt, shame, and burden. Those things will only create more stress and anxiety for you and your significant other. It will be frustrating. At times you won't be able to clean, cook, and otherwise be very engaged with your home responsibilities.

Your children, relatives, friends, and significant other will sometimes miss you and you'll miss them.

There's nothing easy about benzo withdrawal. But it *will* pass.

Laughter

Good humor is another simple but potentially profound tool for recovery. Laughter has a curious affect upon our emotional health and can quite literally reduce anxiety and depression, as well as release feel-good chemicals in our brain.

The more you laugh, the better you'll feel.

Of course, there's nothing funny about going through benzo withdrawal. It's horrible. The symptoms alone make it almost impossible to smile, let alone laugh. And the prolonged mental state of anxiety/depression/stress has left us feeling numb and blank. So how *can* we laugh?

For me, I watched a ton of stand-up comedy via Netflix, and I also watched a lot of comedy films. I remember watching the film *What About Bob* around sixty-two times while going through my withdrawal. I'd often put the film on in the evening before I went to sleep, waking up in the middle of the night (as I usually did several times) and put the film back on. It helped.

Eventually, I was able to laugh, and I did get therapeutic value from this simple routine. It might have been fleeting, but I'll take it. Not only did it give me a moment of relief, but it was healthy for my brain chemistry as well.

I viewed watching comedy shows/films/standup daily as a kind of exercise and therapeutic technique.

These comedy sessions really helped me, but with a little effort, we can find humor in just about anything. However, I'm not asking you to find humor in your situation, I'm just asking that you try regularly to engage in something that might make smile or maybe even laugh.

Art Therapy

Art is such a wonderfully instinctive phenomenon that can be so very healing. As such, art therapy is one of my favorite topics.

This therapy has been around for some years now, since at least the 1960s. Art therapy was initially difficult to quantify, and therefore to scientifically demonstrate its effectiveness in treatment. For that reason, some professionals haven't taken it very seriously over the years.

However, attitudes are changing.

Today, art therapy is used in many settings, including prisons, hospitals, clinics, and various mental health centers.

Art therapy is distinctly different than *therapeutic art making*, which lacks the more self-explorative and existential focus, as well as the focus on accurately interpreting events and symbols in our life.

In other words, therapeutic art making is less structured and grounded in psychological theory of treatment.

However, even therapeutic art making has been shown to result in symptom reduction. In this section, I use both terms interchangeably.

So, how effective *is* art therapy?

This creative technique has been shown in a number of studies to be quite effective in pain management, and is used in hospitals to treat cancer patients, resulting in less opiates and benzodiazepines needed to alleviate symptoms.

Art therapy is used in prison settings with inmates to treat anxiety, depression, stress, and trauma. It also helps to rehabilitate maladaptive behavior.

Statistically, there are 3 times more severely mentally ill people in prisons than are found in state hospitals.

Additionally, prisons are a breeding ground for neurosis and maladaptive behaviors. Art therapy has proved to be quite effective in treating mental illness amongst inmate populations resulting in money saved on costs for prescriptive medications, and antisocial or self-harm behavior.

Another interesting phenomenon of this technique amongst inmates, as identified by Dr.

Gousak (a specialist in art therapy's use in correctional settings) is that art therapy also appears to influence locus of control. This resulted in inmates taking more responsibility for the events in their life. Locus of control is a term in personality psychology that observes how a person internalizes or externalizes the events in their life. In other words, to what degree they have control over events in their life.

This is key in ones ability to take reasonability. With a strong internal locus of control, an individual focuses too heavily upon their ability to affect the events in their life. They overly blame themselves for not being able to control uncontrollable events. Conversely, someone with too much external locus of control instead supports the belief that events are a result of external factors, and that they are helpless and therefore cannot be blamed for their success and failures.

Art therapy was an immensely powerful healing and transformative vessel for me during my benzo wean.

Much of what I've spoken about so far has been focused on biological symptoms, such as anxiety and stress. I've tried to help you see through various examples just how interconnected and perhaps symbiotic, our thoughts can be with our feelings.

What I haven't discussed is the existentialism that also seems to follow the dark cloud of benzo withdrawal.

When I speak on existentialism within this context, I'm looking at the phenomenon of a human being in a foxhole, and how it forces us to take a huge step back, to see outside ourselves, in order to gain some perspective.

What a wonderful instinct that is. The Buddha saw it as a saving grace, this ability to clearly see reality, as it truly is. To see the good and the bad, and to somehow spiritually or consciously elevate above it through a process of self-awareness.

Essentially, that's what the Buddha's teachings were about, though of course it's more intricate than that.

In my opinion, Buddhism isn't a religion; it's the oldest form of psychotherapy known to man.

Religion in its purest uninterrupted essence is essentially psychotherapy.

It is instinct for human beings to come together and celebrate existence, to explore the big questions:

Who am I?
How did I get here?
And where am I going in this ocean of chaos?

The instinct is to confide in one another and to find strength in each other during difficult times.

The instinct is to find or create a symbol of goodness, unconditional love, forgiveness, and all the other virtues we hold close to our heart.

Alternatively, perhaps you do not follow religion, but rather, you find your center through science and through your experiences. Perhaps your friends are your support group, and maybe over a drink and dinner, you occasionally talk about existential topics.

The how and where of the engagement isn't of much importance. What is important is that you're thinking often about yourself, your life, your friends, family, fellow human beings, your country, your planet, and all of creation.

This is a natural instinct within us all, however, and it's a HUGE "however," existentialism is also very frightening at first.

The last thing you want to do is think about your own mortality while you're weaning of a benzo. And indeed, it is **not** the best time to start exploring your biggest existential fears, not when you have an anxiety disorder that's literally attempting to negatively and falsely imprint the details about the events around you.

Things could get quickly overwhelming and misunderstood.

That said, the nature of your condition, namely the prolonged anxiety and depression, is such that it tends to force us into some real existential black holes.

It makes sense that we spend a lot of time thinking about our condition, wondering if we will get better, thinking about and missing our life. It inevitably offers us a different perspective, a very disjointed and disconnected perspective at that.

What does any of this have to do with art therapy?

Everything. Art therapy is about tapping into our unconsciousness and pulling out information about our condition, our environment, and ourselves.

Before a thought becomes conscious, it is unconscious.

Scientists have now proven this using advanced technology; showing that our brain processes things faster than we can comprehend. There is a discrepancy between the unconscious and the conscious articulation.

Additionally, a lot of our psychological nature as human beings is to sustain a balance within our psyche. Consequently, when avenues in our psyche feel attacked, or are unable to process difficult stimulus, it tends to revert to some unconscious defense mechanism.

They are sort of like roadblocks between the truth and you.

Art therapy becomes like a fishing pole that drops a hook deep into the waters of the unconscious, hooking something big and bringing it back up to the surface for us to identify, interpret, and understand.

Art therapy can help you understand some of the hidden things about yourself, and it can give a voice to your complicated feelings. When we accomplish this, we open ourselves to a cathartic experience, a sort of internal mental/emotional purging.

Art is very liberating in that way, a fact that most artists treasure deeply.

You may be thinking, but I'm not good at art?

You don't have to be. You're not planning to sell out a gallery in Los Angeles. You're just looking to have an enjoyable creative experience, using supplies hands on, and hopefully discovering a safe and vulnerable space from which you can work through some tough emotions.

The primary focus should be on the joy that comes with art making, journaling, and other creative outlets.

You can accomplish this in a number of ways, through a number of mediums. The key will be finding which is most enjoyable for you.

While I was tapering, I enjoyed sitting outside and painting the nature scenes that I saw around me, en plein air. I didn't worry too much about how intricate they were, I didn't seek perfection, I just tried to imitate the shapes, colors, tones, and textures that surrounded me in the moment.

This also was a good exercise in forcing myself to look for beauty within nature, rather than focusing on the negatives of my situation.

Sometimes I'd sit outside, or near a window, and sketch in my notebook. Other times I'd write poetry in the bathtub. My guitar was also a good companion on many nights.

However, life after benzo is a unique thing, an emotional rollercoaster, and a systematical re-alignment of several aspects of our life.

Art therapy, writing, and music, were portals of psychotherapy for me, places where I was able to safely explore, interpret, and understand the dynamic components of who I am, currently, and not only who I have been up until this point. It's a phase of rediscovery, which we will explore more in the final pages of this book.

As I said, if you're considering art therapy, or therapeutic art making, don't be concerned with searching for deeper meaning within your work. Do not get lost looking for or creating connections in your work.

Rather, just create for the sake of creating. Allow yourself a moment of escape.

Music Therapy

Music can have a profound impact on our emotions, thus we can use music to help regulate our emotions: to calm us down when we are upset, to lift our mood when we are depressed, to relax us when we are stressed and tense.

Whenever I was feeling particularly down or depressed during my tapering, I would turn on music that was positive and upbeat, such as reggae. When I couldn't sleep I would listen to atmospheric music and nature sounds. If I was anxious, I might put on some classical music.

However, you'll want to be very mindful of your choices, as this wonderful tool can also work against us.

I didn't think of music as being a therapeutic tool on my belt, at least not initially. Instead, I did what many of us do when we are feeling depressed and anxious, I listened to music that resonated with the pain I was going through. While this can certainly be cathartic, too much of this melancholy melody can really lead us even further into depression, as it has a way of emotionally locking us into those feelings.

In the earlier days of my recovery, without realizing, I had been listening to the same sad music for months on repeat before a friend kindly pointed it out to me. From there forward, I became very aware and changed the music I was listening to. With this one simple adjustment, I experienced noticeable relief, things felt a little less dark, a little more manageable.

The Last Dose

The day finally arrives. It felt like it never would come.

You had worried it was impossible, that you wouldn't be able to do it, but now it's here and you did it. The last dose, which probably at this point looks like a tiny little chip of a pill.

In the end, I had a prescription bottled that looked like a rainbow, filled to the top with little pieces of Valium, different milligram tablets, from blue, to orange, to green, to white.

Probably around 2 or 3 months prior to my last wean, I had really started to feel noticeably better, though it was still certainly no walk in the park. The last week almost snuck up on me, and when I took the last dose I felt a mix of emotions.

Part of me felt like I had just climbed Mount Everest, and in a small way, I had.

However, the other side of me was left feeling a bit vulnerable, without any support. I had leaned on this crutch for so long and now I wondered if I was really ready to throw it away.

I still suffered considerably from anxiety, though I was not longer displaying signs of agoraphobia. I was also able to focus on college and be more socially interactive. I was noticeably better but was I truly ready for this next step?

I still battled occasional panic attacks, usually triggered by lack of sleep and too much caffeine. Somewhat self-induced, I must admit. And I still got overwhelmed and felt panicky in crowded places when I couldn't be near an exit.

Large shopping centers were still a nightmare for me after my last dose of benzo.

This is when I realized that I had to enter a whole new level of lifestyle changes that would facilitate my continued recovery.

These essentially were not new practices or therapies, but rather, I had to get more serious with the things I had already been doing. I had to be more disciplined, and I had to put myself out there more, quite literally.

I had to face my fears daily.

This was such an important realization in my personal journey that I wanted to close this book on it, as I think it could be just as important to you. I feel very strongly that this one thing could mean the difference between continued success in achieving freedom from anxiety, and freedom from the need to depend on benzodiazepine, or not.

On the day of your last dose, congratulate yourself. You deserve it.

Now comes life after benzodiazepine, and that life is still a work in progress. Pre-existing conditions still remain, and benzo prolapsed withdrawal may still be lingering.

Our second part of the battle begins after our last dose.

Stigmatization & Healthy Self Image

One of the most common byproducts of dealing with mental health issues is the fear of stigmatization, and in a major way, this is a personal phenomenon—a self-created problem.

Typically, as adults, the people around us are rather understanding about mental health problems. Things like depression and anxiety alone affect almost 20% of the United States population, 18 years of age and older, every year. That's one in five people, making it pretty common.

Most people experience anxiety and depression at some point in their lifetime, often repeatedly to some degree. Yet, less than 40% of those suffering ever seek professional help.

Part of the reason for this is the fear of stigma.

However, if you were prescribed a benzo, then there is likely some underlying mental health condition that it was intended to treat.

So, we've already had to observe the stigma of seeing a doctor for our condition, be it depression, anxiety, trauma, or other. And we've already had to accept the diagnosis and treatment.

We had to find the courage to be able to acknowledge within ourselves, "I am suffering _____ and that's okay. It's very normal, and it in no way defines who I am."

Still, when you're going through benzo recovery, it is almost impossible at times to see the forest for the trees. On top of our pre-existing diagnosis, we now must add "benzo dependence recovery" on top of the list. It can seem a little self-defeating, if we allow it.

As I've said before in this book, there is no room for that kind of thinking while we are healing, or thereafter for that matter.

Healthy self-image is of immense importance for self-esteem, healthy mood regulation, and for managing clarity in our perception. Consequently, and imperatively, we must work towards achieving this healthy self-image. We accomplish this through daily positive self-talk, and through the practice of striving to see the bigger picture always.

We are not what we went through or what we are currently going through. This is but a profound speed bump. We are forever changed by our experiences, but we don't have to be defined by them.

Sure, we can allow our experiences to have a stigmatic affect upon the way we perceive our self, and we can give in to the negative self-talk. Or we can instead see this as a profound opportunity for growth and healing, of self-discovery.

We are not a victim. We are a survivor. We are strong.

Standing on the other side of this experience today, I am left with a sense of renewal, pride, and duty.

I no longer worry about stigmatization, because I see myself as a fighter, a survivor, and an advocate for benzo awareness. I feel very blessed in a sense to be able to share my experiences and my knowledge in psychology to help ease the suffering of others as they go through benzo recovery.

It is true. There is a mental health stigma in the United States. Some people can be very cruel, and some people just do not understand it. But many people do.

Ultimately, all we can control is how *we* perceive ourselves, and how we choose to treat ourselves. I recommend we use a delicate and graceful touch.

Life After Benzodiazepines

This is another one of those more obvious topics in the book that might carry a voice of caution, and hopefully some profound advice.

Life after benzo is not something we simply allow to happen.

We do not merely take the last dose, throw away the old prescription bottle, and just go back to life.

Unlike many drugs, benzo withdrawal symptoms can linger for quite a while after our last dose. No one likes to talk or think about this, but it's true.

If you're expecting to take your last dose, and then within a couple weeks you're going to bounce back to your old self, I regret to inform you that it's unlikely, and here's why.

Not only have you been undergoing benzo withdrawal, which has had a profound chronic chemical disruptive affect upon your neurobiology, and not only do withdrawal symptoms remain after our last dose for a short period (in some rare cases even years), but we have to remember one important fact, a fact of which we may have lost sight of during this chemical battle we've been in.

And that fact is, whatever mental illness or biological hang-up we had prior to taking the benzo will still be there after the benzo.

In fact, it's likely to be much worse because all we've been doing is sedating it, and now it's reemerging, without medication, with no therapy, and we are going to have to deal with it. There's no way around it.

After my last dose, I spent the next few months feeling like I had actually gotten a little bit worse. It wasn't severe, but I felt the extra anxiety and depression, insomnia, obsessive-compulsivity in my thoughts, eating, and other behaviors.

There was no doubt that I was going to have to wait a little longer for these last symptoms to work their way out, and they eventually did. One by one, things cleared up.

The social anxiety I had was a combination of biological disposition (anxiety/depression runs in my family), and some maladaptive behaviors I picked up that were perpetuating anxiety.

I also I had to take better charge of my life. I

needed to pick myself up and get myself off this little island of despair that I had been stuck on.

I accomplished this by doing a lot of things that made me uncomfortable, some of which gave me extreme anxiety.

In a synchronous twist, it was my responsibilities to my psychology program that helped pull me the rest of the way out of my anxious rut, giving me the tools to help sustain a better quality of life after benzos.

One of my biggest fears in life has always been flying. Being in the sky is majestic, but it has also always been terrifying for me. Maybe it's the lack of control, though I think I'd be just as afraid to steer the plane as I am sitting in an aisle seat.

Due to education responsibility I had to fly several times to residencies and conferences during my 2nd year off benzos. I spent a total of 44 hours in the sky. Talk about exposure therapy!

This was terrifying, but it drove a very familiar theme home for me— that it's all going to be okay. I made it.

I made it through 44 hours in the sky. I made it, all the way off benzos. I made it through college and managed a career. Yes. There was life after benzo, but yes, I was going to have to work hard at fixing the underlying anxiety disorder I had.

The final piece for me was joining a gym. When I first joined the gym, I was still dealing with the persisting social anxiety issues. I didn't like being in crowded large places like malls, grocery stores, and airports, let alone the gym, where everyone seem perfect, well adapted, and beautiful.

Even a few years after my last benzo dose I still battled with those preexisting issues, stuff that come before benzos, stuff that was tied to my anxiety and depression, stuff that was made all the more intense by my benzo experiences.

I had a negative self-image, and I was still working out some regret and even some anger that I carried regarding what I had gone through on benzo. I felt robbed of part of my life, and I was angry to go through all of that and still discover that I had this pre-existing anxiety disposition.

Joining the gym helped me become more social, and it gave me something to work towards that made me feel better. I felt better physically, which had a tremendous effect upon my anxiety/depression symptoms, and sleep problems, but I also had more self-confidence and started to view myself less negatively.

Eventually, pretty much all of my social anxiety disappeared, and I am now comfortable in airports, malls, grocery stores, concerts, and other crowded places.

The things that helped me the most are shared throughout this book, and often shared several times on purpose. A healthy perspective is critical for our recovery, because it puts everything in balance and allows us to gain clarity.

There it is all before us.

We probably had anxiety/depression/trauma/ sleep disorder prior to taking a benzodiazepine.

We are likely to still deal with these symptoms after our last dose of benzo, and we should be expecting this challenge.

The good news is, there are things we can do to aid in our recovery from benzo dependence, and there are things we can do to gain control of our anxieties and/or depression, but it requires hard work, and hard commitment on our behalf.

It requires self-educating.

It requires us to put ourselves in uncomfortable places while we desensitize through exposure.

It will require lifestyle changes in the way we eat, sleep, exercise, and interact with our environments.

It will take a lot, but in the end, you can make it, and each year you can get better. I won't fool you with false hope, and I don't feel that I've done that in this book. I've done nothing but tell you how long and hard this road is, but I'm not going to lie to you either.

We do get better.

There is life after benzodiazepine.

Acknowledgements

A special thank you to those that served as a lighthouse in my darkest hour.

With love to my mother, and to my Lilith, both of whom tolerated me at my worst and helped me focus on brighter days. Thank you.

To my mentor and cosmic friend, Dr. Brian Deery (Bodhi), who dragged me out of the house regularly for coffee, and conversation. What a blessing it was to have a brilliant friend that's both a comedian and psychologist. Thank you.

To Alex & Dan for keeping me active with fishing and Hapkido. Thank you.

To my good friend Davina, fellow writer & artist, and all-around incredible editor. You helped me actualize this endeavor. Thank you.

And to Gambit, my now departed wolf companion, for your unconditional love. You'd wake me up each morning with a smile, nudging me and encouraging me to get out of bed. Thank you.

About the Author

David Powers is a developing psychologist, currently working on his doctoral degree in Clinical Psychology, with a special focus in Art Therapy, Jungian psychology, Applied Behavioral Analysis and Dialectical Behavioral Therapy.

In addition to his education and career as a psychologist, David is a neo-renaissance artist, a photographer, writer & musician who loves coffee, wolves, and nature.

David currently resides in Florida.

Printed in Great Britain
by Amazon